SOUPS AND STEWS

For Slow Cooker, Stovetop, Oven and Pressure Cooker

Sandra Rudloff

BRISTOL PUBLISHING ENTERPRISES

San Leandro, California

A **nitty gritty**® Cookbook

Printed in the United States of America.

ISBN: 1-55867-269-9

Cover design: Frank J. Paredes
Cover photography: John A. Benson
Food stylist: Susan Devaty
Illustrator: Caryn Leschen

CONTENTS

1   The Best Cooking Method for Your Soup or Stew

3   Stocks

12   Stovetop Soups and Stews

59   Slow Cooker Soups and Stews

94   Pressure Cooker Soups and Stews

118   Oven-Cooked Soups and Stews

150   Index

THE BEST COOKING METHOD
FOR YOUR SOUP OR STEW

Warm, comforting, nutritious soups and stews can be prepared by several different methods, depending on time, ingredients available and convenience for the cook. They can be prepared quickly on the stovetop or in a pressure cooker, or cooked more slowly in the oven or the slow cooker.

In general, when choosing a cooking method, the recipes in this book fall into one of the following categories:

Stovetop soups and stews contain ingredients need more attention or have a short cooking time.

Slow cooker (or Crock-Pot®) soups and stews have all the ingredients combined at the beginning and are left to cook mostly undisturbed, a real convenience for a cook who is busy or away for the day. A slow cooker is energy-efficient compared to an oven, and keeps the kitchen cooler on a hot day.

A pressure cooker is ideal for making soups and stews with tougher cuts of meat, and for saving time and fuel, especially when cooking bean-based soups and stews. This is a "no peek" method of cooking, so many recipes cannot be made in a pressure cooker. Stovetop or slow cooker cooking options are noted at the end of these recipes.

Oven-cooked soups and stews work for larger cuts of meats and recipes that need minimal attention during cooking. They tend to cook in a shorter amount of time than in the slow cooker because the temperatures are higher.

TOP YOUR SOUPS WITH COLOR, TEXTURE AND FLAVOR

Besides croutons and grated cheese, there are many other toppings that will enhance your soups. Try some of these the next time you serve soup.

Vegetables

Slice or chop vegetables or cut them into matchstick-sized strips.

*Carrots	White mushrooms
*Turnips	Spinach
Pea pods	Zucchini
Red bell peppers	Chives
Green Onions	Parsley

*Blanch for 1 minute before using.

Other Toppers

Chopped hard-cooked egg	Sour cream
Crushed tortilla chips	Crumbled cooked bacon
Slivered almonds	Grated cheeses
Chopped peanuts or walnuts	Fried won ton strips

STOCKS

Stocks enhance the flavor of both soups and stews. They can be the base of the recipe, or used in place of water. True, you can purchase cans of chicken, beef, fish and vegetable stocks at your local market. But you can also make up large batches fairly inexpensively, and keep smaller portions in your freezer for instant use.

Commercial stocks tend to be over-salted, even if you buy the reduced sodium type. Never use bouillon cubes or powder, as they are mostly just salt and chemicals. If you do use a canned stock, do not add any salt to your soup or stew until you have tasted it just before serving.

4 Chicken Stock
6 Chicken Stock #2
7 Beef Stock
8 Fish Stock
9 Vegetable Stock
10 Vegetable Stock #2

CHICKEN STOCK

This stock is very easy and economical to make, and the flavor is significantly better than canned broth. Instead of using a carcass from a cooked chicken, chicken thighs and legs (the least expensive parts) are used here. You can buy frozen leg or thigh pieces, frequently sold in 5 or 10 lb. bags, and keep them on hand just for making stock. Browning the chicken pieces first gives this stock a depth of flavor and color different from other recipes, where chicken parts and vegetables are placed in water and then brought to a boil. It is important to cook the chicken until all sides are a deep golden brown. Don't worry about bits of skin or meat that may stick to your pot — they will loosen up when you add the water. This recipe makes about 4 cups of stock. If you have a large stockpot, make up a larger quantity and freeze for up to 6 months.

1 chicken leg
1 chicken thigh
4 cups water
$\frac{1}{2}$ tsp. salt

1 small carrot, cut into chunks
1 stalk celery, cut into 2-inch pieces
$\frac{1}{2}$ yellow onion, thickly sliced

In a medium stockpot, brown leg and thigh over medium heat. Cook until chicken is browned on all sides, about 20 minutes, keeping pot covered at all times except when turning chicken.

Add remaining ingredients and bring to a boil. Cover, reduce heat to low and simmer for 1 hour.

Pour stock through a wire strainer and discard vegetables, chicken skin and bones. Reserve chicken meat for another use or chop coarsely and add to stock. Remove fat from top surface of stock prior to using or freezing. Refrigerate and use within 3 days, or freeze for up to 6 months.

CHICKEN STOCK #2

Try to make a habit of making stock every time you have a chicken carcass after a meal. Using the carcass plus any remaining skin and meat (such as the back, wings or wing tips) will give you a light-colored but full-flavored stock. If you use only the carcass, you won't get a very "chicken-y" broth. And don't throw away the neck from the giblets package: if you cook it along with your carcass, you'll get even more flavor. All stocks and broths freeze well — you may never have to buy canned stocks again.

1 chicken carcass, plus neck from
   giblets package
4 cups water
1/2 bay leaf
1 small carrot, cut into chunks

1 stalk celery, cut into 2-inch pieces
1/2 yellow onion, unpeeled and thickly
   sliced
1/4 tsp. salt

Combine all ingredients in a medium stockpot and bring to a boil. Cover and reduce heat to low. Simmer for at least 2 hours, or until bones separate easily.

Pour stock through a wire strainer and discard vegetables, chicken bones and skin or meat. Remove fat from top surface of stock prior to using or freezing. Refrigerate and use within 3 days, or freeze for up to 6 months.

BEEF STOCK

The best thing about making beef stock is how truly inexpensive it can be. Go to your market and ask someone in the meat department for soup bones. I've received them free, or paid up to 20 cents a pound for them. You can make a gallon of beef stock for sometimes less than $1.00. You can also do this with some meaty bone from cuts such as short ribs, shank portions or back ribs if you can't purchase soup bones. This makes it a bit more expensive, but again you get a lot for your money.

3 lb. beef soup bones
16 cups water
2 bay leaves
1 cup chopped carrots

1 cup chopped celery
1 yellow onion, chopped
½ tsp. salt

In a large stockpot, brown beef bones. Add water and all remaining ingredients and bring to a full boil. Reduce heat to low, cover and simmer for 3 hours.

Pour stock through a wire strainer. Refrigerate and use within 3 days, or freeze for up to 6 months. Skim off fat before using or freezing.

FISH STOCK

Fish heads — I don't normally come in contact with a lot of these! I also don't have fish skeletons lying around. Fish stock recipes often call for mostly heads, skeletons and scraps; they really aren't that practical. So I created this fish stock by using very inexpensive fish pieces, either filleted or with bones. Fish gives up its flavor to the broth very quickly, so a long simmer time isn't needed. One additional note about fish stocks: do not use strongly-flavored fish such as salmon. Use only the mildest-tasting fish to create a stock that will work with most soups and stews.

1 lb. mild white-fleshed fish
   (cod, haddock or similar)
1 yellow onion, peeled and chopped

2 stalks celery, chopped
$\frac{1}{2}$ tsp. salt
6 cups water

Cut fish into 2-inch pieces. Combine all ingredients in a medium-to-large stockpot. Bring to a boil, cover and reduce heat to low. Simmer for 30 minutes.

Pour stock through a wire strainer and press lightly to extract as much juice as possible, especially from fish pieces. Refrigerate and use within 3 days, or freeze for up to 6 months.

VEGETABLE STOCK

Makes about 2 quarts

Vegetable stock should be fairly neutral in flavor. Not just any vegetables work for making stock, though. Strong-flavored vegetables such as broccoli or Brussels sprouts will make your stock taste primarily of that vegetable. This stock is a good substitute for chicken or fish broth.

8 cups water
1 clove garlic, chopped
2 yellow onions, chopped
4 carrots, chopped
4 stalks celery, chopped
2 russet potatoes, thickly sliced
1 cup chopped white mushrooms
$\frac{1}{2}$ tsp. salt

Combine all ingredients in a large stockpot. Bring to a boil, cover and reduce heat to low. Simmer for 1 hour.

Pour stock through a wire strainer and press lightly to extract as much juice as possible. Refrigerate and use within 3 days, or freeze for up to 6 months.

VEGETABLE STOCK #2

This is a roasted vegetable stock. Its bolder flavor can be used as you would use beef stock.

2 yellow onions, halved
2 roma tomatoes, halved
4 carrots, cut into 2-inch pieces
4 stalks celery, cut into 2-inch pieces
2 potatoes, cut into 1-inch-thick slices
3 cloves garlic, peeled
1 cup whole white mushrooms
$1/4$ cup olive oil
16 cups water
$1/2$ tsp. salt

Heat oven to 400°.

Place onions and tomatoes cut-side up in a large pan or roaster. Arrange carrots, celery, potatoes, garlic and mushrooms around onions and tomatoes. Drizzle olive oil over all vegetables. Place vegetables in oven and roast until browned, about 45 to 60 minutes.

Place vegetables and any liquid in pan into a large stockpot. (Note: If you have bits of vegetables stuck to pan, or if there are some browned juices, add 1 cup water to pan and return to oven for 10 minutes. Scrape up any bits and add liquid and vegetable bits to stockpot.) Add water and salt and bring to a boil over high heat. Reduce heat to low, cover and simmer for 1 hour.

Pour stock through a wire strainer and press lightly to extract as much juice as possible. Refrigerate and use within 3 days, or freeze for up to 6 months.

STOVETOP SOUPS AND STEWS

The most common way of making soups and stews is on the stovetop. It allows you the flexibility of adding ingredients when you want to and frequent stirring and tasting.

The recipes in this section all use stovetop cooking to their advantage. These soups and stews are either a bit more labor-intensive or have shorter cooking times than other cooking methods. Some recipes have the vegetables cooked just to crisp-tender, which you cannot control with any other cooking method.

14   North Beach Minestrone
16   Italian Meatball Soup
18   Chicken Minestrone
19   Real Old-Fashioned Chicken
      Noodle Soup
20   Chicken Mushroom Noodle Soup

21   Chinese Cabbage and Noodle
      Soup
22   Creamy Chicken and Broccoli
      Soup
23   Sausage and Pasta Soup
24   Winter Vegetable Soup

25 Roasted Corn Chowder
26 Summer Vegetable Chowder
27 Beef and Barley Soup
28 Baja Black Bean and Shrimp Soup
29 Seafood Soup
30 Shrimp Bisque
32 Mulligatawny Soup
33 Ham and Potato Soup
34 Won Ton Soup
36 Cheddar Cheese Soup
37 Broccoli and Cheddar Soup
38 Lentil and Spinach Soup
39 Old World Cabbage Soup
40 Creamy Mushroom Soup
41 Wild Mushroom and Wild Rice Soup

42 Creamy Chicken and Corn Soup
43 Cream of Spinach Soup
44 Red Chicken Curry
45 Chicken El Cid
46 New Orleans Jambalaya
48 Irish Stew
50 Lamb Stew With Olives and Rosemary
51 Greek Lamb Stew
52 San Francisco Cioppino
54 Chicken Cacciatore
55 Chicken Gumbo
56 Blanquette of Veal
58 Hungarian Pork Stew

NORTH BEACH MINESTRONE

This is my mother's minestrone, and she really did learn how to make it when she lived in the North Beach area of San Francisco.

2 tbs. olive oil
1/2 lb. beef stew meat, diced
2 qt. beef stock
1 can (28 oz.) ready-cut tomatoes
1 can (15 oz.) kidney beans or white beans
2 cups cubed potatoes
2 cups cubed banana squash
1 cup chopped carrots
1 cup chopped celery
1 cup chopped zucchini
3 cups shredded Napa cabbage
1 tsp. dried basil
1/2 tsp. dried oregano
1 tsp. garlic salt
2 cups small cooked pasta shapes (such as tiny shells)
freshly grated Parmesan cheese, optional

Heat olive oil in a large stockpot. Add beef and cook until browned. Add stock and tomatoes, and bring to a boil. Cover and simmer for 30 minutes, until beef is tender.

Add beans, potato, banana squash and carrots. Cover and simmer for 20 minutes. Add all remaining ingredients except pasta. Cook until all vegetables are tender but not mushy, about 15 minutes. Add pasta and heat for an additional 5 minutes.

Serve hot, with freshly grated Parmesan cheese to sprinkle on top, if desired.

ITALIAN MEATBALL SOUP

This soup does take a bit of work, as you make and cook the meatballs first. But the effort is worth it for a hearty soup. The meatballs are great for other uses as well, so you can make up extra and freeze them. When cutting Swiss chard or kale, be sure to use only the leaves, as the stems are too chewy for this soup.

MEATBALLS

½ lb. ground pork
½ cup fresh breadcrumbs
1 egg

2 tbs. beef stock
½ tsp. dried basil
½ tsp. salt

SOUP

8 cups beef stock
2 large potatoes, peeled and chopped
½ yellow onion, chopped
1 clove garlic, chopped

Meatballs
4 cups Swiss chard or kale leaves
freshly grated Parmesan cheese,
   optional

MEATBALLS

Heat oven to 400°. Mix all ingredients together. Shape into ¾-inch balls. Place meatballs on a cookie sheet and bake until well browned, about 20 minutes. Remove from cookie sheet and drain on paper towels. Set aside.

SOUP

In a large stockpot, combine stock, potatoes, onion, garlic and meatballs. Bring to a boil and reduce heat to low. Cover and simmer for 30 minutes. Add chard or kale and simmer for 5 minutes, until greens are tender but still bright. Just before serving, top with grated Parmesan cheese, if desired.

CHICKEN MINESTRONE

Servings: 6–8

This is a lighter version of traditional minestrone, but with lots of the same vegetables and flavors.

6 cups chicken stock
1 cup chopped zucchini
1 cup chopped carrots
1 cup chopped fresh green beans, cut into ½-inch pieces
1 can (14.5 oz.) Italian-style chopped tomatoes
1 can (15 oz.) great Northern beans
2 cups shredded Napa cabbage
2 cups chopped cooked chicken
1 cup chopped banana squash
½ tsp. dried basil
½ tsp. dried oregano

Combine all ingredients in a large stockpot. Bring to a boil, reduce heat to low and simmer until all vegetables are tender, about 30 minutes.

REAL OLD-FASHIONED
CHICKEN NOODLE SOUP

Not at all like soup from a can, this is just a simple warming soup that is perfect for a rainy day.

8 cups chicken stock
1 cup minced cooked chicken
2 carrots, minced
2 stalks celery, minced
1 cup uncooked thin egg noodles

In a large stockpot, bring chicken stock, chicken, carrots and celery to a boil. Reduce heat to low and simmer for 20 minutes.

While soup is simmering, cook noodles according to package directions. Rinse with cool water and drain. Add drained noodles to soup and serve immediately.

CHICKEN MUSHROOM NOODLE SOUP

Servings: 6–8

This is not your grandmother's chicken noodle soup! The taste is more "grown up" than a basic chicken noodle soup, thanks to the mushrooms and sherry. I used white mushrooms when I made this soup, but it will be even more dramatic if you use a mixture of fresh mushrooms, such as brown, portobello, shiitake, oyster and others.

1 boneless, skinless chicken breast half
2 tbs. butter
1 yellow onion, chopped
1 lb. mushrooms, sliced

3 stalks celery, chopped
8 cups chicken stock
1/2 cup dry sherry
1 cup uncooked wide egg noodles

Cut chicken breast into tiny pieces. Melt butter in a large stockpot over medium heat. Add chicken and cook until it begins to brown. Add onions, mushrooms and celery. Continue to cook, stirring almost constantly, until mushroom liquid is released and mushrooms begin to brown slightly.

Add stock and sherry and bring soup to a boil. Cover and reduce heat to low. Simmer for 30 minutes, until chicken meat is tender.

While soup is simmering, cook noodles according to package directions. Drain pasta when done and set aside. Add cooked pasta and serve.

CHINESE CABBAGE AND NOODLE SOUP

Servings: 4–6

Asian buckwheat noodles are also called "chunka soba" and can be found in all Asian markets and many supermarkets. The shredded cabbage strands look like noodles when cooked.

6 cups chicken stock
1 tbs. soy sauce
1-inch piece fresh ginger, peeled and sliced
2 cups chopped cooked chicken
4 cups shredded Napa cabbage
1/2 lb. buckwheat noodles, cooked according to package directions

In a large stockpot, mix together stock, soy sauce, ginger and cooked chicken. Bring to a boil, cover and simmer for 10 minutes. Remove ginger pieces.

Add cabbage and noodles and cook only until cabbage is wilted. Serve immediately.

CREAMY CHICKEN AND BROCCOLI SOUP

Servings: 4–6

Cream, cheddar cheese and lots of fresh broccoli make this soup perfect for lunches or dinners.

2 tbs. butter
2 tbs. flour
4 cups chicken stock
5 cups chopped fresh broccoli
2 cups chopped cooked chicken
1 cup heavy cream
1 cup grated sharp cheddar cheese

Melt butter over medium heat in a large stockpot. Add flour and stir until smooth. Stirring constantly, add stock and continue to cook until slightly thickened. Add broccoli and chicken. Reduce heat to low, cover and simmer for 5 to 10 minutes, until broccoli is tender, but not limp.

Remove from heat. Stir in cream and cheese. Return to heat and stir until cheese has melted and is well mixed into soup.

SAUSAGE AND PASTA SOUP

Feel free to use any shape pasta here. You can also use flavored pasta or three color pasta for a delicious addition. Be sure to cook the pasta "al dente" (al dente means slightly chewy, cooked until firm to the bite), and don't let soup simmer too long after adding, or else your pasta will be overcooked.

4 hot or mild Italian sausages in
   casings
2 stalks celery, chopped
2 carrots, chopped
1 yellow onion, chopped

8 cups chicken stock
2 cups chopped peeled tomatoes
2 cups cooked tiny shell pasta, cooked
   "al dente"

Place sausages in a large stockpot. Cook sausages over medium heat until browned and cooked through. Remove from pot to cool slightly. Pour off excess fat from pot.

Return pot to stove. Add celery, carrots and onion and sauté until onions begin to brown. Add stock and tomatoes to pot and bring to a boil, scraping up the bottom to loosen any browned bits. Reduce heat to low, cover and simmer for 20 minutes. While soup simmers, cut sausages into 1/4-inch-thick slices. Return sausage slices to soup and simmer for 10 minutes. Add cooked pasta and simmer for 5 minutes.

WINTER VEGETABLE SOUP

You can get all the fresh vegetables for this soup easily and inexpensively in the middle of winter.

8 cups chicken, beef or vegetable stock
1/2 cup chopped yellow onion
1 cup chopped celery
1 cup chopped carrots
1/2 cup chopped peeled turnips
1 cup chopped peeled potato
2 cups shredded green cabbage
1/2 tsp. salt

Combine all ingredients in a large stockpot. Bring to a boil over high heat. Cover and reduce heat to low. Simmer for 15 minutes or until potatoes are tender.

ROASTED CORN CHOWDER

Cooking the corn under the broiler give this soup a bit of a smoky taste.

6 ears corn, husked and cleaned
3 tbs. vegetable oil
3 slices bacon, chopped
1/2 yellow onion, chopped

4 cups vegetable stock or water
2 medium potatoes, peeled and
  chopped
2 cups half-and-half

Preheat broiler. Rub corn with vegetable oil and set on a cookie sheet. Place under broiler and cook until corn begins to brown, about 5 minutes. Turn ears over and brown other sides. Remove from oven and let cool. When cool, scrape off kernels. Reserve corn cobs for soup.

In a large stockpot over medium heat, brown bacon until crisp. Remove from pot and drain all fat from pot. Add onions and sauté until translucent. Add stock, potatoes, corn cobs and corn kernels to pot. Bring to a boil and reduce heat to low. Cover and simmer for 30 minutes, or until potatoes are tender.

Remove corn cobs from soup and discard. Add half-and-half and cooked bacon to soup and serve.

SUMMER VEGETABLE CHOWDER

Servings: 6–8

This soup features all the wonderful produce from your summer garden, or from the local farmer's market.

3 large potatoes, peeled and chopped
1 yellow onion, chopped
4 cups water or chicken stock
4 ears corn on the cob
2 stalks celery, chopped
2 medium zucchini, chopped

1 red bell pepper, seeded and chopped
1 cup shelled fresh peas
1 cup seeded, chopped tomatoes
1/2 tsp. salt
2 cups milk, or to taste

In a large stockpot, combine potatoes, onion and water or stock. Bring to a boil and then simmer until potatoes are tender, about 20 minutes. Lightly mash potatoes with a spoon to break up some of them — it doesn't need to be smooth.

Remove kernels from corn cobs and discard cobs. Add corn, celery and zucchini to pot. Cook for 15 minutes over medium-low heat. Stir in red bell pepper and peas. Cook for an additional 5 minutes. Add tomatoes, salt and milk and continue cooking only until soup is hot.

BEEF AND BARLEY SOUP

Servings: 6–8

Not too many people use barley anymore, but I like the chewy texture it adds to soup.

2 tbs. olive oil
1 lb. beef stew meat, cut into tiny
  pieces
10 cups beef stock
1/2 cup barley
2 carrots, sliced
2 turnips, peeled and chopped
2 stalks celery, chopped
1 tsp. salt

Heat oil in a large stockpot over medium-high heat. Add beef and cook until browned. Add stock, barley, carrots, turnips, celery and salt, and bring mixture to a boil. Reduce heat to low and simmer for 1 hour, until barley is done and beef is tender.

BAJA BLACK BEAN AND SHRIMP SOUP

Servings: 4–6

If you think all bean soups are heavy, try this one. The fresh taste of bay shrimp and cilantro lighten the heavy bean taste.

2 cans (16 oz. each) black beans
2 stalks celery, chopped
1 green bell pepper, seeded and chopped
1 red bell pepper, seeded and chopped
5 cups chicken stock
2 cups chopped tomatoes
1 tsp. ground cumin
$\frac{1}{2}$ lb. bay shrimp
2 tbs. chopped fresh cilantro

Combine all ingredients except shrimp and cilantro in a large stockpot. Bring to a boil over medium heat. Cover, reduce heat and simmer for 30 minutes.

Stir in shrimp and cilantro. Serve immediately.

SEAFOOD SOUP

Lighter than a cioppino or bouillabaisse, this tomato-based soup features whatever fresh fish you can find. You want about 1 1/4 pounds of fish fillets and the fillets should be about 1/2-inch thick, so use whatever looks good at the market. Skip the shellfish in their shells (such as clams or mussels) and save them for a stew. This is meant to be an easy-to-eat soup!

1/2 lb. cod fillets
1/2 lb. red snapper fillets
1/4 lb. salmon fillets
1/2 cup olive oil
1 yellow onion, chopped
1 cup white wine

2 cups canned tomatoes, finely
  chopped
4 cups fish stock or water
1/2 lb. small cooked shrimp
1/2 lb. cooked crabmeat
grated zest of 1 lemon

Cut fillets into small, bite-size pieces. Heat olive oil in a large stockpot over medium heat. Add onion and sauté until golden. Add wine and bring to a boil, scraping up any browned bits on bottom of pot. Add tomatoes, stock and fish pieces. Bring to a boil. Cover, reduce heat to low, and simmer for 20 minutes. Stir in cooked shrimp, crab and lemon zest. Continue to cook until heated through and serve.

SHRIMP BISQUE

Real shrimp bisque uses a stock made of the shells of the shrimp — lots of shells. This gives the stock an intense shrimp flavor. This is a version that will give you a deep shrimp taste, but is much easier to make.

1/4 cup butter
1 lb. prawns in shells
1/2 yellow onion, peeled and chopped
1/2 cup white wine
6 cups fish or vegetable stock
1/2 cup uncooked white rice
2 cups peeled, seeded, chopped tomatoes
1 tsp. salt
1/4 lb. cooked small shrimp
1 cup heavy cream

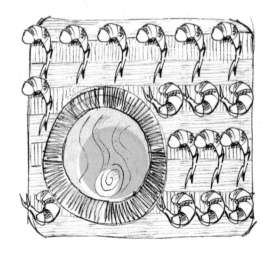

In a large stockpot, melt butter over medium heat. Add prawns (in their shells) and onion. Sauté until prawns are well cooked. Add wine, stock, rice, tomatoes and salt. Bring soup to a boil, cover and reduce heat to low. Simmer for 20 minutes or until rice is tender.

Remove cooked prawns from soup. Peel prawns and remove tails; discard shells and tails.

Coarsely chop prawns. Return prawns to pot. Purée soup, in batches if necessary, in a blender until smooth. Return to pot.

Bring soup to a boil. Add shrimp and heavy cream. Stir to mix and serve immediately.

Note: Do not let soup boil after cream has been added.

MULLIGATAWNY SOUP

Servings: 6–8

This Indian soup is flavored with curry and made creamy with the addition of unsweetened coconut milk or cream. It is fun to serve with a variety of toppings, such as finely chopped apples, raisins, chopped peanuts, etc.

1 lb. boneless, skinless chicken breasts
2 tbs. vegetable oil
1 yellow onion, chopped
1 clove garlic, minced
5 cups chicken stock
1 tbs. curry powder, or to taste

1/2 tsp. powdered dried ginger
2 whole cloves
1 cup diced carrots
1 cup cooked white rice
1 cup heavy cream or unsweetened coconut milk

Cut chicken into tiny pieces. Heat oil in a large stockpot over medium heat. Add chicken and cook until meat is white but not browning. Add onion and garlic and continue to cook until onions are golden.

Add stock, curry powder, ginger, cloves and carrots. Bring to a boil, cover and reduce heat to low. Simmer for 30 minutes.

Remove cloves from soup. Add white rice to soup and heat through. Stir in cream or coconut milk and serve immediately.

HAM AND POTATO SOUP

Chunks of ham and potato are surrounded by a potato puréed soup. A great way to use up some leftover holiday ham!

6 cups water
4 large potatoes
3 cups chopped cooked ham
1 yellow onion, chopped
2 stalks celery, chopped
1 tsp. salt
2 cups milk

Place water in a large stockpot. Peel and chop 3 of the potatoes and add to water. Bring to a boil over high heat. Cover and simmer until potatoes are falling-apart tender, about 20 minutes.

Purée soup in batches and return to pot. Peel and coarsely chop remaining potato and add to pot. Add ham, onion, celery and salt. Bring to a boil over medium heat; cover and reduce heat to low. Simmer until potato chunks are tender, about 30 minutes, depending on the size of your chunks. Add milk until you reach desired thickness, and heat for another 5 minutes.

WON TON SOUP

Restaurant won ton soup will pale in comparison to this version. The won tons are filled with a light-tasting mixture of chicken and shrimp and the stock is flavorful and loaded with vegetables. Won ton skins are found in most supermarkets in the refrigerated or produce section.

BROTH

8 cups chicken stock
1-inch piece fresh ginger, peeled and sliced
2 tbs. soy sauce
1/4 cup sherry

WON TONS

1/2 cup minced cooked chicken
1/2 cup minced bay shrimp
2 tbs. minced green onions
1/2 tsp. ground dried ginger
1/2 tsp. soy sauce
1 egg
36 won ton skins

SOUP

Broth
Won Tons
$\frac{1}{2}$ cup thinly sliced carrots
$\frac{1}{2}$ cup thinly sliced zucchini
$\frac{1}{2}$ cup Chinese pea pods, washed and ends trimmed
$\frac{1}{2}$ cup white mushrooms, sliced

To make stock: In a large stockpot, combine chicken stock, fresh ginger, soy sauce and sherry. Bring to a boil, reduce heat and simmer over low heat for 15 minutes while you make won tons.

To make won tons: In a small bowl, mix together chicken, shrimp, green onions, ground ginger, soy sauce and egg. Place about $1\frac{1}{2}$ teaspoons of the filling in center of each won ton skin. Fold over to make a triangle and seal edges with a bit of water, pressing lightly. Continue until all filling is used. Set assembled won tons aside on waxed paper.

To make soup: Remove ginger slices from stock. Bring stock to a full boil over high heat. Gently drop in won tons, carrots, zucchini, pea pods and mushrooms. Stir gently and return to a full boil. Reduce heat to low and continue to cook for 5 minutes. Serve immediately.

CHEDDAR CHEESE SOUP

This creamy soup can be made into a very hearty meal by adding 1 or 2 cups of chopped cooked ham just before serving. It is also wonderful when topped with some crumbled crisp bacon.

2 tbs. butter
2 tbs. flour
6 cups milk
2 cups grated sharp cheddar cheese
1/4 tsp. dry mustard

In a large stockpot, melt butter over medium heat. Add flour and, using a wire whisk, mix in until smooth. Pour milk into sauce, stirring constantly. Return to heat and cook until mixture begins to thicken, stirring constantly. Do not let milk boil. Add cheese and dry mustard and stir constantly until melted. Serve immediately.

BROCCOLI AND CHEDDAR SOUP

Broccoli and cheddar are a favorite pairing. I like to purée only part of the broccoli, so I have some chunks of broccoli in the soup. But if you prefer a smoother soup, purée all of the broccoli.

2 tbs. butter
1 yellow onion, chopped
1 large potato, peeled and chopped
4 cups chopped broccoli

2 cups water or chicken stock
$1/2$ tsp. salt
4 cups milk
2 cups grated cheddar cheese

In a large stockpot, melt butter over medium heat. Add onion and sauté until translucent. Add potato, broccoli and water or stock. Reduce heat to low, cover and simmer until potato is very tender, about 15 minutes.

Puree soup in batches until smooth. For a more chunky soup, you can also puree about $3/4$ of the soup, and leave the remainder. Return soup to pot. Add salt, milk, and cheese and cook over medium heat, stirring constantly. Heat only until hot; do not boil.

LENTIL AND SPINACH SOUP

Servings: 8

This is how my Italian grandmother used to make lentil soup. You could also add some chunks of kielbasa or cooked ham to make this even heartier.

2 cups lentils
8 cups water or vegetable stock
1 carrot, chopped
3 stalks celery, chopped
1 yellow onion, chopped
1 potato, peeled and chopped
1 can (14 oz.) ready-cut tomatoes
$1/2$ tsp. dried sage
2 cloves garlic, minced
1 tsp. salt
$1/2$ lb. spinach, washed and cut into $1/2$-inch strips

Combine all ingredients, except spinach, in a large stockpot. Bring to a boil, cover and reduce heat. Simmer until lentils are tender, about 45 minutes. Add spinach and simmer for another 5 minutes.

OLD WORLD CABBAGE SOUP

Servings: 4–6

This soup is hearty and inexpensive to make. Serve with a rustic bread for an old-fashioned meal.

1 head Savoy or Napa cabbage, shredded
1 yellow onion, chopped
2 carrots, chopped
2 potatoes, peeled and chopped
6 cups chicken stock

Combine all ingredients in a large stockpot. Bring to a boil over high heat and reduce heat to low. Cover and simmer for 30 minutes, or until potatoes are tender.

CREAMY MUSHROOM SOUP

Mixed mushrooms, and lots of them, make this soup very different from canned cream of mushroom soup. My favorite wild mushrooms to use in this soup are chanterelles. This soup is very rich and filling, so it can be a main dish when served with bread and some cheeses.

1/4 cup butter
1/2 lb. white mushrooms, finely chopped
2 leeks, white part only, thinly sliced
1 lb. wild mushrooms, chopped
4 cups chicken or vegetable stock or water
1 cup heavy cream

Melt butter in a large stockpot over medium heat. Add chopped white mushrooms and sauté until liquids are released and they begin to brown. Add leeks and continue to cook until leeks are translucent.

Add wild mushrooms and stock. Bring to a boil and reduce heat to low. Simmer, uncovered, for 15 minutes. Remove from heat and add cream. Do not return to heat. Serve immediately.

WILD MUSHROOM AND WILD RICE SOUP

The tastes of wild mushrooms and wild rice go together very well — this makes a special soup perfect for guests.

6 cups chicken or vegetable stock
1 cup wild rice
2 oz. dried porcini mushrooms
2 tbs. butter
$\frac{1}{2}$ lb. white mushrooms, sliced
$\frac{1}{2}$ lb. wild mushrooms (oyster, chanterelle, etc.), sliced

Combine stock and wild rice in a large stockpot. Bring to a boil over medium-high heat. Reduce heat to low, cover and simmer for 30 minutes.

While rice is cooking, soak dried mushrooms in hot water for 15 minutes. Remove from water, pat dry and chop finely.

Heat butter in a large skillet. Add white and wild mushrooms and sauté until liquids are released and mushrooms begin to brown. Add cooked mushrooms and dried porcini mushrooms to pot. Stir to mix, cover and simmer for 10 minutes. Serve immediately.

CREAMY CHICKEN AND CORN SOUP

Servings: 4–6

Many Chinese restaurants offer a version of this soup. This is thicker than a chowder because of the addition of white rice. Top with a sprinkling of slivered green onions.

1 cup shredded cooked chicken
1 can (17 oz.) creamed corn
1 cup corn kernels, frozen, fresh or canned
5 cups chicken stock
$1/2$ cup uncooked white rice
1 tsp. soy sauce

Combine all ingredients in a large stockpot. Bring to a boil over medium heat, stirring frequently. Reduce heat and simmer until rice is very tender, about 30 minutes. Add additional stock if you prefer a thinner soup.

CREAM OF SPINACH SOUP

If you like creamed spinach, you'll love this soup.

3 cups chicken stock
2 medium potatoes, peeled and chopped
4 cups spinach, leaves only
2 cups half-and-half
$\frac{1}{2}$ tsp. freshly ground nutmeg

Combine chicken stock and potatoes in a large stockpot. Bring to a boil and cook until potatoes are very tender, about 20 minutes. Remove from heat and add spinach. Stir to mix, cover and let stand for 5 minutes.

Purée potatoes, spinach and cooking stock in batches. Return puréed mixture to pot and heat to boiling. Remove from heat and stir in half-and-half and nutmeg. Serve immediately. If soup is not hot enough, return to medium heat and continue to warm slowly, but never allow soup to boil. Stir frequently while heating.

RED CHICKEN CURRY

Curry and tomatoes pair up for a spicy chicken stew. Serve over hot white or brown rice for a complete meal.

2 tbs. vegetable oil
1 chicken, cut into 8 pieces
1 yellow onion, chopped
1 green bell pepper, cut into chunks
2 cans (14½ oz. each) stewed tomatoes
1 tbs. curry powder
1 tsp. garlic salt

Heat oil in a medium stockpot over medium-high heat. Add chicken and sauté until chicken is just beginning to brown, about 15 minutes. Reduce heat to medium-low.

Add onion, bell pepper, tomatoes, curry powder and garlic salt. Stir to mix and simmer for 30 minutes, or until chicken is tender.

CHICKEN EL CID

This stew gets a bright and fresh taste by adding cilantro just before serving.

2 tbs. olive oil
1 frying chicken, cut into 8 or more serving pieces
1 yellow onion, sliced
2 cloves garlic, minced
1 green bell pepper, seeded and coarsely chopped
3 cups ready-cut tomatoes
$\frac{1}{2}$ tsp. Tabasco Sauce
$\frac{1}{2}$ tsp. garlic salt
$\frac{1}{2}$ cup chopped fresh cilantro

In a large Dutch oven or stockpot, heat oil over medium heat. Add chicken and cook until browned on all sides. Add onion, garlic, bell pepper, tomatoes, Tabasco Sauce and garlic salt. Stir to mix. Reduce heat to low and simmer for 1 hour.

Remove from heat. Stir in fresh cilantro and serve immediately.

NEW ORLEANS JAMBALAYA

Servings: 8–10

Jambalaya is one of those "kitchen sink" recipes — you can throw in so many different things and still have a great meal. Here I've used chicken, pork spareribs, garlic sausage and prawns; but you can also add in chunks of ham, hot and spicy sausages, even oysters. Don't cook this until all the liquid is gone; as soon as the rice is tender, remove from heat and serve.

2 tbs. olive oil
1 frying chicken, cut into 8 or more
   serving pieces
2 lb. pork spareribs, cut into 2-inch
   "mini-riblets"
1 lb. garlic sausage, cut into
   1/2-inch-thick slices
1 yellow onion, chopped
1 cup chopped celery

1 cup chopped green bell pepper
2 cloves garlic, minced
2 cups long-grain rice
1 tsp. red pepper flakes
1 tsp. salt
4 cups chicken or vegetable stock
1 lb. tomatoes, chopped
1 lb. prawns, peeled and deveined
grated zest of 1 lemon

In a large Dutch oven or stockpot, heat olive oil over medium heat. Add chicken and spareribs and fry until meats are well browned. Remove from pot and set aside.

Add sausage, onion, celery, bell peppers and garlic to pot and sauté until onions are translucent, about 5 minutes. Add rice and stir well to coat rice with oil. Cook for another 5 minutes until rice begins to turn translucent.

Return chicken and ribs to pot and add red pepper flakes, salt, stock and tomatoes. Stir to mix, reduce heat to low and cover. Simmer for 10 to 15 minutes, or until rice is almost tender. Add prawns and lemon zest to pot and fold in gently. Cover, return to heat and cook until rice is tender and prawns are cooked, about another 5 to 10 minutes.

IRISH STEW

Here is another old, traditional stew with lots of variations. The rule of Irish stew is that you have to use lamb and potatoes — anything else is up to you. This recipe adds baby carrots and a touch of herbs. Serve with a nice rustic bread for a great winter meal.

3 tbs. flour
1 tsp. salt
2 lb. lamb chunks, about 1½-inch cubes (breast or boned shoulder work well)
¼ cup vegetable oil or bacon drippings
1 yellow onion, coarsely chopped
3 large potatoes, peeled and cut into 1½-inch chunks
3 cups water
¼ tsp. dried rosemary
¼ tsp. dried thyme
1 cup baby carrots

Mix flour and salt together in a large plastic bag. Add lamb chunks and shake to coat well.

Over medium heat, heat oil in a Dutch oven or large stockpot. Add meat chunks and cook until browned on all sides. Add onion, potatoes, water, rosemary and thyme to pot. Scrape off any browned bits attached to bottom of pot. Bring stew to a boil; cover and reduce heat to low. Simmer for 1 hour, stirring occasionally. Add carrots to pot; cover and continue to cook for 30 minutes.

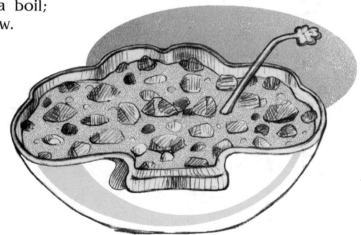

LAMB STEW WITH OLIVES AND ROSEMARY

Servings: 4–6

If you like their strong taste, you can use kalamata olives here instead of black olives — or try a mixture of half of each type. Roasted potatoes make a nice side dish to the flavors of this stew.

2 tbs. olive oil
2 lb. lamb stew meat
1 clove garlic, minced
1/2 tsp. dried rosemary, or 1 tsp. chopped fresh
2 cups beef stock
1 can (7 oz.) pitted black olives

In a Dutch oven or stockpot, heat oil over medium-high heat. Add lamb and garlic and sauté until browned. Add rosemary, stock and olives, and bring to a boil. Cover and reduce heat to low. Simmer for 1 hour, or until meat is tender.

GREEK LAMB STEW

Servings: 4–6

Fresh lemon juice, added to this stew at the very end, gives it a light taste. This is a stew that is perfect any time of year.

1/4 cup olive oil
2 lb. lamb stew meat
2 cloves garlic, minced
2 tsp. dried oregano
1/2 tsp. salt
3 cups beef or chicken stock
1/2 cup freshly squeezed lemon juice

In a Dutch oven or stockpot, heat oil over medium-high heat. Add lamb and garlic and sauté until browned. Add oregano, salt and stock and bring to a boil. Cover and reduce heat to low. Simmer for 1 hour, or until meat is tender. Stir in lemon juice, and serve immediately.

SAN FRANCISCO CIOPPINO

This stew should be made with whatever fish you like — there is no real "recipe" for this wonderful stew, with the exception of using fish and shellfish, tomatoes, wine and garlic. The rest is up to you: here is my favorite version. Be sure to serve with lots of fresh French bread!

1/4 cup olive oil
5 cloves garlic, minced
2 yellow onions, chopped
2 cups white wine
1/2 cup chopped fresh flat-leaf parsley
2 green bell peppers, seeded and
   chopped
2 cans (28 oz. each) plum tomatoes
2 cups chicken stock
1 tbs. hot pepper sauce (such as
   Tabasco Sauce)
1 tbs. dried oregano

1 tbs. dried basil
1 tsp. salt
1 lb. swordfish fillet, cut into 1-inch
   chunks
1/2 lb. salmon fillet, cut into 1-inch
   chunks
1 lb. medium shrimp, peeled and
   deveined
24 hard-shell clams, scrubbed
1 lb. cleaned calamari
1 lb. cooked cracked crab

In a large stockpot, heat olive oil over medium heat. Add garlic and onion and sauté until golden brown. Add wine and scrape bottom of pot to loosen any browned bits. Add parsley, bell peppers, tomatoes, stock, hot pepper sauce, oregano, basil and salt. Bring to a boil, reduce heat to low and cover. Simmer for 30 minutes.

Add swordfish and salmon. Cook until tender, about 15 minutes. Add shrimp, clams, calamari and crab and cook until clams have opened and all fish is cooked, about 10 minutes more.

CHICKEN CACCIATORE

Servings: 4–6

This is a comfort food for me, especially when served with steaming hot polenta. If you don't like polenta, serve with some wide egg noodles.

1/4 cup olive oil
1 frying chicken, cut into 8 or more
   serving pieces
2 cloves garlic, minced
1 yellow onion, sliced
1/2 cup white wine

1 green bell pepper, seeded and sliced
1/2 lb. mushrooms, sliced
2 cans (28 oz. each) plum tomatoes
1/2 tsp. dried oregano
1/2 tsp. dried basil
1/2 tsp. salt

Heat oil in a large stockpot or Dutch oven over medium heat. Add chicken and cook until golden brown. Remove chicken and set aside. Add garlic and onion to pot and sauté until onions begin to brown. Add wine and scrape up browned bits from bottom of pan.

Return chicken to pot. Add bell peppers, mushrooms, tomatoes, oregano, basil and salt and stir to mix. Reduce heat to low, cover and simmer for 45 minutes.

CHICKEN GUMBO

You can't make gumbo without okra. This can be considered both a stew — because of the large pieces of chicken — and a soup. If you don't want large pieces of chicken, you can use about 2 lb. boneless, skinless breasts or thighs, cut into chunks, instead.

2 tbs. vegetable oil
1 frying chicken, cut into 8 or more
   serving pieces
1 yellow onion, chopped
1 cup chopped tomatoes
1 cup sliced okra, about ½-inch slices

½ cup chopped green bell pepper
½ cup chopped celery
1 carrot, chopped
8 cups chicken stock
½ tsp. dried thyme
1 bay leaf

Heat oil in a large Dutch oven or stockpot over medium heat. Add chicken and cook until browned. Add onions and continue cooking until onions are lightly browned. Add all remaining ingredients and increase heat to high. Bring to a boil, reduce heat, cover and simmer for 1 hour. Remove bay leaf before serving.

BLANQUETTE OF VEAL

This is a French cream-based veal stew; the tender veal is surrounded by a rich cream sauce and mushrooms. Pair this with lighter side dishes, such as steamed vegetables or a rice pilaf.

2 whole cloves
1 yellow onion, peeled
2 lb. veal stew meat
4 cups chicken stock or water
1 carrot, chopped
4 peppercorns
2 tbs. chopped fresh parsley
1 bay leaf
12 small white onions, peeled
2 cups sliced mushrooms
3 tbs. butter
3 tbs. flour
2 tbs. lemon juice
2 egg yolks
3/4 cup heavy cream

56   STOVETOP SOUPS AND STEWS

Push cloves into whole onion. Place onion, veal, stock, carrot, peppercorns, parsley and bay leaf into a large stockpot or Dutch oven. Bring stock to almost boiling over medium heat. Reduce heat to low and simmer, covered, for 1 hour.

Remove veal from stock and set in a bowl. Strain stock, discarding vegetables and herbs. Return stock to pot. Add white onions and simmer until tender, about 10 minutes. Remove onions to veal bowl. Add mushrooms to stock and cook until tender, about 3 minutes.

Increase heat to medium and reduce stock down to 2 cups. While reducing stock, melt butter in a small saucepan. Add flour and stir to make a smooth sauce. Add 1 cup of the reduced stock to sauce, stirring constantly until smooth. Pour sauce into remaining stock, stirring constantly. Return veal and vegetables to pot, reducing heat to low.

Stir together lemon juice, egg yolks and cream. When meat is hot, stir in cream mixture. Stirring constantly, cook just long enough to heat through. Do not boil or overcook or sauce will curdle.

HUNGARIAN PORK STEW

Pork, potatoes, and cabbage stew together for a hearty one-pot meal.

$1/4$ cup olive oil
3 lb. pork stew meat
1 yellow onion, sliced
1 medium head Savoy or Napa
    cabbage, coarsely shredded
3 large potatoes, peeled and cut into
    large chunks

1 cup white wine
3 cups chicken stock
1 bay leaf
1 clove garlic, peeled and left whole

Over medium heat, heat oil in a large stockpot or Dutch oven. Add pork and cook until browned. You will need to do this in batches. As meat is browned, remove to a bowl. Add onion, cabbage and potatoes to pot, stirring to coat vegetables in remaining oil. Add wine and stock and scrape up any browned bits on bottom of pan.

Return pork to pot and add bay leaf and garlic. Bring to a boil, reduce heat to low, cover and simmer for 1 hour. Remove cover. Remove bay leaf and garlic and discard. Continue to cook for an additional 30 minutes to reduce stock.

SLOW COOKER SOUPS AND STEWS

Slow cooker soups and stews have the advantage of unattended cooking. It is the ideal way to combine ingredients in the morning, leave for work, and have a meal waiting for you when you come home.

I have found that slow cookers vary widely in their cooking temperatures — my old slow cooker cooked at about 100° lower than other brands. Low temperature setting is usually 200°, high is usually 300°. Cooking times here are estimates, so you will need to adjust the cooking time based upon your experience with your slow cooker.

You won't see a lot of seafood recipes in this section. Seafood does not do well in the slow cooker, as the long cooking times will toughen almost every type of seafood.

61   Tuscan Bean Soup
62   Texan Bean and Sausage Soup
63   Cal-Mex Black Bean Soup
64   Barley and Pancetta Soup
65   Chunky Split Pea Soup
66   Lentil and Brown Rice Soup

67 Autumn Turkey Soup
68 Wild Rice Soup
69 Hamburger Vegetable Soup
70 Chipotle Chicken Soup
71 Chicken and Stars Soup
72 Potato and Spinach Soup
73 Baked Potato Soup
74 Manhattan Clam Chowder
75 New England Clam Chowder
76 Shrimp Ratatouille
77 Beef Curry With Vegetables
78 Rich Beef Stew With Gravy
79 Italian Herbed Beef
80 Steak and Mushroom Stew

81 Belgian Beef Stew
82 Sweet and Smoky Beef Stew
83 Chili Verde
84 Pork and Apple Stew
85 Northern Italian Pork Stew
86 Chicken and Dumplings
88 Chicken With Sun-dried
    Tomatoes
89 Garlic Chicken
90 Cran-Apple Chicken
91 Fireball Chili
92 California Chili
93 Chicken Chili

TUSCAN BEAN SOUP

Servings: 6–8

Rosemary and smoked ham hocks are used to flavor this white bean soup. Serve with some crusty French bread to dip into the soup. Spooning chopped fresh tomatoes on top makes a pretty presentation.

1 cup dried white beans, such as Great Northern
4 cups water
4 cups chicken stock
1 ham hock
3 cloves garlic, minced
2 tsp. chopped fresh rosemary
1 yellow onion, chopped
1 large potato, peeled and finely chopped
1 tsp. salt

Pick over beans and soak in water overnight. Rinse and drain.

Place soaked beans and all other ingredients in the slow cooker. Cover and cook on high heat until beans are tender, about 6 to 8 hours. Remove ham hock. Discard bone, skin and fat. Chop meat, return to soup and serve.

TEXAN BEAN AND SAUSAGE SOUP

Servings: 6–8

Spicy chorizo sausage is used here, but you can also use kielbasa-type sausage too. Just use ½ lb. of the kielbasa sausage, diced. No need to cook it; just add it with all the other ingredients. Try topping this soup with salsa, sour cream or slices of avocado.

1 cup dried black beans
½ lb. chorizo sausage
4 cups water
4 cups chicken stock
2 stalks celery, chopped
1 yellow onion, minced
1 cup commercially prepared salsa
½ tsp. ground cumin
1 tsp. salt

Pick over beans and soak in water overnight. Rinse and drain.

In a medium skillet, brown chorizo. Drain fat and place cooked sausage in the slow cooker. Add soaked beans and all remaining ingredients. Cover and cook on high heat until beans are tender, about 6 to 8 hours.

CAL-MEX BLACK BEAN SOUP

Many bean soups rely on ham, bacon and sausage for flavor, because the beans themselves aren't very flavorful. Here, a small amount of meat is used, but the soup gets a lot of its flavor from the herbs and vegetables. Top each bowl with a spoon-ful of sour cream or salsa.

4 cans (15 oz. each) black beans
1 can (15 oz.) refried black beans
2 yellow onions, minced
2 red bell peppers, chopped
2 cans (4 oz. each) mild green chiles, chopped
3 cloves garlic, minced
1 cup chopped cooked ham
8 cups stock, any kind, or water
1 tbs. ground cumin
1 tsp. freshly ground black pepper
1/2 cup minced fresh cilantro
2 tbs. brown sugar, packed

Combine all ingredients in the slow cooker. Stir to mix well. Cover and cook on low heat for 6 to 8 hours.

BARLEY AND PANCETTA SOUP

Pancetta (Italian bacon) is simmered with barley for a thick and hearty soup. Serve with a light green salad.

1/2 lb. pancetta, cut into tiny cubes
1 yellow onion, minced
1 cup minced celery
1 1/4 cups pearl barley
6 cups chicken stock
freshly grated Parmesan cheese, optional

In a medium saucepan, cook pancetta over medium heat for 5 minutes. Add onion, celery and barley and sauté until onion is translucent, about 10 minutes. Transfer all to the slow cooker.

Add stock to slow cooker and cover. Cook on low heat for 4 to 6 hours, or until barley is tender. Top with Parmesan cheese, if desired.

CHUNKY SPLIT PEA SOUP

I like the combination of creamy pea soup with chunks of meat and vegetables in it. Use either yellow or green split peas in this recipe — they both taste great. If the soup is really thick after the cooking time, add water (or chicken or vegetable stock), about 1/2 cup at a time, until you reach desired consistency. You can also use chicken stock or vegetable stock here.) Try topping this soup with crumbled, crisply-cooked bacon or grated cheddar cheese.

8 cups water
2 ham hocks
1 lb. split peas
2 carrots, cut into 1/4-inch thick slices
3 stalks celery, cut into 1/4-inch thick slices
1 yellow onion, coarsely chopped
1 large potato, peeled and finely chopped

Combine all ingredients in the slow cooker. Cover and cook on high heat until peas are soft and tender, about 4 to 6 hours.

Remove ham hock. Discard bone, skin and fat. Chop meat, return to soup and serve.

LENTIL AND BROWN RICE SOUP

Servings: 8–10

I like to serve this with a hearty "peasant-style" bread — and it goes well with a tall glass of very cold beer!

10 cups stock, any kind
2 cups lentils
2 carrots, chopped
1 yellow onion, chopped
2 stalks celery, chopped
1 can (14.5 oz.) tomatoes
1 1/2 cups brown rice
1 lb. garlic sausage, chopped

Combine all ingredients in the slow cooker. Cook on high heat for 6 hours, or until brown rice is tender.

AUTUMN TURKEY SOUP

This is an ideal way to use a post-Thanksgiving turkey; the soup is a far cry from Thanksgiving tastes and textures. So when you are tired of reheating your leftover turkey and mashed potatoes, try this soup. If you can, make a stock using the turkey carcass. Just follow the recipe for chicken stock, using the turkey carcass instead. If you cannot find the tiny new potatoes called creamers, you can use red potatoes cut into $1/2$-inch pieces.

4 cups chopped cooked turkey
8 cups chicken or turkey stock
4 cups shredded Swiss chard
1 lb. tiny red new potatoes ("creamers")
2 cups chopped carrots
2 cups chopped celery
2 cups chopped mushrooms
$1/2$ lb. banana squash, peeled and cut into 1-inch pieces

Combine all ingredients in the slow cooker. Cover and cook on low heat until all vegetables are tender, about 4 to 6 hours.

WILD RICE SOUP

Here is another great autumn soup. Try topping this soup with browned slivered almonds. The toasted nut taste complements the wild rice flavor.

1/4 cup butter
1/2 cup wild rice
6 cups chicken stock
1/2 yellow onion, minced
1/2 cup minced celery
2 cups finely chopped cooked chicken
1/2 lb. winter squash, peeled, seeded and cut into 1/2-inch cubes

Melt butter in a small skillet. Add rice and sauté for 10 minutes over low heat. Transfer rice and butter to the slow cooker.

Add stock, onion, celery, chicken and squash to slow cooker. Cover and cook until rice and vegetables are tender, about 4 to 6 hours.

HAMBURGER VEGETABLE SOUP

Kids really like this simple vegetable soup — it has all the favorite kid vegetables, in a mild beef stock.

1 lb. lean ground beef
4 stalks celery, chopped
4 carrots, chopped
2 potatoes, peeled and chopped
1 cup frozen peas
1 cup frozen corn kernels
6 cups beef stock
$1/2$ tsp. dried oregano

In a medium skillet, brown ground beef over medium-high heat.
Drain fat and place cooked beef in the slow cooker. Add all remaining ingredients and stir to mix. Cover and cook on low heat for 6 to 8 hours.

CHIPOTLE CHICKEN SOUP

Smoky chipotle peppers add heat to this Mexican-style soup. These smoked jalapeño peppers are very hot, so use only ½ a pepper if you don't like your food too spicy. Top with broken corn chips and a spoonful of sour cream.

2 tbs. vegetable oil
2 boneless, skinless chicken breast
 halves
1 yellow onion, chopped
2 cloves garlic, minced
2 cups corn kernels, frozen

2 medium red- or white-skinned
 potatoes, peeled and chopped
6 cups chicken stock
1 chipotle pepper
½ tsp. salt

Heat oil in a medium skillet over medium heat. Add chicken and cook until golden brown on all sides. Remove from pan and set aside to cool slightly. When cool enough to handle, chop into small pieces. Transfer chicken to the slow cooker.

Place onion and garlic in skillet and cook until onion begins to brown. Transfer onion and garlic to slow cooker. Add carrots, potatoes, stock, chipotle pepper and salt. Stir to mix. Cover and cook on low heat for 6 to 8 hours. Remove chipotle pepper prior to serving.

CHICKEN AND STARS SOUP

Servings: 6–8

This comfort soup has the pasta added at the last moment, so the stars stay firm. The slow-cooked stock with tiny bits of vegetables will warm you on the coldest winter day.

8 cups chicken stock
2 cups finely chopped cooked chicken
4 carrots, finely chopped
1/2 yellow onion, minced
2 stalks celery, finely chopped
4 oz. uncooked pastina or stars

Combine all ingredients, except pasta, in the slow cooker. Stir to mix. Cover and cook on low heat for 6 to 8 hours.

Just prior to serving, cook pasta according to package directions. Drain pasta and add to soup. Serve immediately.

POTATO AND SPINACH SOUP

Servings: 4–6

If you use frozen chopped spinach for this soup, you can more easily squeeze out excess liquid. If you use fresh, chop the spinach first and then steam or boil lightly. Once cooked, press out all the liquid you can before adding to the soup.

4 medium potatoes, peeled and finely chopped
1 yellow onion, chopped
1 cup chopped cooked smoked ham
3 cups chicken stock
$\frac{1}{2}$ tsp. salt
1 pkg. (9-oz) chopped frozen spinach
1 cup half-and-half

Combine potatoes, onion, ham, stock and salt in the slow cooker. Cover and cook on low heat for 6 to 8 hours, or until potatoes are very soft.

Squeeze spinach until no liquid remains and add to soup. Add half-and-half and stir to mix well. Increase heat to high and cook for an additional 15 minutes.

BAKED POTATO SOUP

Next time you bake potatoes for dinner, throw a few more in, and you can have this wonderful soup the next day. I've always liked potatoes with skins on, and this method keeps the skins on the chunks of potato, instead of them separating.

6 large baked potatoes
1 cup chopped celery
1 yellow onion, minced
6 cups chicken stock
1 tsp. salt
2 cups half-and-half, or to taste

Cut potatoes into 1-inch chunks (do not peel). Place potatoes, celery, onion, chicken stock and salt in the slow cooker. Cover and cook on low heat for 6 to 8 hours. Lightly press potatoes to break them up a bit. Stir in half-and-half and heat through, about 15 minutes.

MANHATTAN CLAM CHOWDER

Servings: 4–6

Some people are very adamant about which type is better, Manhattan (tomato-based) or Boston/New England (cream-based). Both can be easily made in the slow cooker. Here is the tomato-based soup.

4 slices bacon
1 yellow onion, chopped
2 stalks celery, minced
2 carrots, chopped
3 medium potatoes, peeled and chopped
1 bay leaf
1 can (28 oz.) stewed tomatoes, crushed
4 cups vegetable or fish stock
4 cans (6½ oz. each) clams, with juice

Brown bacon in a skillet over medium heat. Drain bacon and crumble. Add bacon to the slow cooker.

Add all remaining ingredients to slow cooker. Cover and cook on low heat for 8 hours. Remove bay leaf before serving.

NEW ENGLAND CLAM CHOWDER

This creamy version of clam chowder has the cream added in the last hour of cooking so it will not curdle.

4 slices bacon
1 yellow onion, chopped
4 stalks celery, minced
3 medium potatoes, peeled and chopped
$1/4$ cup chopped fresh parsley
2 cups vegetable or fish stock
4 cans ($6^1/_2$ oz. each) clams, with juice
4 cups half-and-half

Brown bacon in a skillet over medium heat. Drain bacon and crumble. Add bacon to the slow cooker.

Add all remaining ingredients, except half-and-half, to slow cooker. Cover and cook on low heat for 8 hours. Increase heat to high. Add half-and-half. Cook for 10 minutes to heat through.

SHRIMP RATATOUILLE

This has the flavors of ratatouille without all the vegetables. The sauce cooks slowly, and the shrimp are added at the end so they don't overcook. Serve with a simple rice pilaf.

1 yellow onion, chopped
3 cloves garlic, minced
1 green bell pepper, seeded and chopped
1 red bell pepper, seeded and chopped
2 cups peeled, seeded, chopped tomatoes
1 tsp. dried thyme
1 bay leaf
3 tbs. freshly squeezed lemon juice
2 lb. medium to large shrimp, peeled and deveined

Combine all ingredients, except shrimp, in the slow cooker. Cover and cook on low heat for 4 to 6 hours. Add shrimp, stir to mix and replace lid. Continue cooking until shrimp are pink and firm, about 5 to 10 minutes, depending on size of shrimp. Remove bay leaf before serving.

BEEF CURRY WITH VEGETABLES

This is a very spicy curry, not sweet. Serve with some freshly baked bread and honey butter.

3 lb. beef stew meat
2 yellow onions, coarsely chopped
4 carrots, cut into 1-inch pieces
1/4 cup curry powder, or to taste
1 can (14 oz.) ready-cut tomatoes
2 cups beef stock
2 cups frozen green peas

Combine beef, onions, carrots, curry powder, tomatoes and stock in the slow cooker. Cover and cook on low heat for 8 to 10 hours, or high for 6 to 8 hours, until beef is fork-tender.

Add peas and stir to mix. Replace lid and cook for 15 minutes.

RICH BEEF STEW WITH GRAVY

Servings: 4–6

Here is a great way to make a stew with a rich, thick gravy — use a gravy mix! Be sure to cook this on low heat only, or else your gravy will stick to the slow cooker. Try using some different flavors of gravy mixes, such as onion or mushroom.

2 tbs. vegetable oil
2 lb. beef stew meat
1 cup red wine
2 cups water
1 pkg. (1.61 oz.) beef gravy mix
1/2 tsp. dried rosemary

Heat oil in a large skillet over medium-high heat. Add beef in batches and cook until well browned on all sides. Transfer cooked beef to the slow cooker.

When all beef has been browned, add wine to skillet to loosen browned bits from bottom of pan. In a small bowl, mix together beef stock and beef gravy mix, stirring until smooth. Add to wine in skillet and bring to a boil, stirring constantly. Add rosemary to gravy mixture and pour over beef in slow cooker.

Cook on low heat for 4 to 6 hours, or until beef is fork-tender.

ITALIAN HERBED BEEF

Servings: 6–8

This stew starts in the skillet and ends in the slow cooker. The dredging flour used for the beef is also used to thicken the cooking liquid, so you have a thicker sauce.

½ tsp. dried thyme
½ tsp. dried oregano
½ cup flour
2 lb. beef stew meat

2 tbs. olive oil
½ yellow onion, chopped
1 cup red wine
2 cups beef stock

Combine thyme, oregano and flour together in a large locking plastic bag. Add beef and shake to coat. Heat oil in a large skillet over medium-high heat. Shake off excess flour from meat and place in hot oil, being careful not to crowd (you will need to cook meat in a few batches). Brown meat on all sides and transfer to the slow cooker. Reserve 1 tbs. of the flour and herb mixture.

Drain all but 2 tbs. of the fat from skillet. (Add more olive oil if needed to make 2 tbs.) Add onion and sauté until onion softens. Add wine and beef stock and bring to a boil, scraping up any browned bits on bottom of skillet. Pour over beef in slow cooker.

Cover and cook on high heat until beef is tender, about 4 to 6 hours. Mix reserved flour and herb mixture with 2 tbs. water. Stir until smooth. Add to beef stew and cook for 15 minutes to thicken.

STEAK AND MUSHROOM STEW

Servings: 4–6

You can use cooked, leftover steak for this stew — just cook for a total of about 4 hours and skip browning the beef in butter.

¼ cup butter
2 lb. round steak, cut into 1-inch pieces
1 lb. mushrooms, sliced
½ cup sherry
1 yellow onion, chopped
¼ cup chopped fresh parsley
3 cups beef stock
1 bay leaf

Melt butter in a large skillet over medium heat. Add beef in batches and cook until browned. Transfer browned beef to the slow cooker.

When done cooking beef, add mushrooms to skillet. Sauté until mushrooms' liquid is released and they begin to brown. Add sherry and scrape up any browned bits from bottom of pan. Pour sherry and mushrooms into slow cooker.

Add onion, parsley, stock and bay leaf to slow cooker. Cover and cook on high heat for 6 hours. Remove bay leaf before serving.

BELGIAN BEEF STEW

Servings: 8

This stew has hunks of beef simmered with beer and herbs. Make a huge amount of mashed potatoes and let everyone pile potatoes on their plate and spoon this hearty stew on top.

2 tbs. vegetable oil
3 lb. beef stew meat
1 yellow onion, minced
2 cups beer
1 cup beef stock
1 bay leaf
$1/2$ tsp. dried thyme
2 tbs. chopped fresh parsley
1 tbs. Dijon mustard

Heat oil in a large skillet over medium-high heat. Add beef, in batches if necessary, and brown well on all sides. Transfer beef to the slow cooker. Add onions to skillet and cook until onions are translucent. Add onions to slow cooker.

Add beer, stock, bay leaf, thyme, parsley and mustard to slow cooker. Cover and cook on high heat until beef is tender, about 4 to 6 hours. Remove bay leaf before serving.

SWEET AND SMOKY BEEF STEW

Servings: 6–8

Take the flavors of barbecue, slow cook them with beef, and you have this sweet and smoky stew. You can serve this on top of a big baked potato for a Saturday night feast.

2 tbs. vegetable oil
3 lb. beef stew meat
1 yellow onion, finely chopped
3 cloves garlic, minced
4 cups commercially prepared tomato-based salsa
2 cups beef stock
1/4 cup vinegar
1/2 cup brown sugar, packed
1/4 cup Worcestershire sauce
2 tsp. Liquid Smoke

Heat oil in a large skillet over medium heat. Add beef in batches and cook until browned. Transfer browned beef to the slow cooker.

Add all remaining ingredients to slow cooker. Cook on high heat for 6 to 8 hours, until beef is fall-apart tender.

CHILI VERDE

This is a simple pork stew, with a spicy green sauce. Serve with warm tortillas and let people eat the stew like a taco, or serve with rice. Tomatillos are found in the produce section of many supermarkets. You will need to remove the outer husk before using.

¼ cup vegetable oil	4 cups chopped tomatillos
3 lb. pork stew meat	2–4 jalapeño chile peppers, chopped
4 cloves garlic, minced	1 tsp. ground cumin
1 yellow onion, chopped	½ tsp. salt
3 cups chicken stock	

In a medium skillet, heat oil over medium heat. Add pork in batches and cook until browned on all sides. As meat cooks, transfer browned pieces to the slow cooker.

When all pork has been browned, add garlic and onion to pan. Sauté until onion is translucent. Add stock to pan and scrape up any browned bits on bottom. Pour stock and onion mixture into slow cooker.

Add tomatillos, jalapeño peppers, cumin and salt to slow cooker. Stir to mix, cover and cook on high heat until pork is fall-apart tender, about 6 hours.

PORK AND APPLE STEW

Servings: 4–6

Pork and apples complement each other so well it seems a natural to cook them together. This stew is slightly sweet and perfect for autumn meals.

2 lb. pork stew meat
2 large green apples, cored and cut into quarters
½ cup chopped yellow onion
2 tbs. maple syrup
1 cup chicken stock
1 tbs. cornstarch
¼ cup chicken stock

Place pork, apples, onion, maple syrup and 1 cup stock in the slow cooker. Stir to mix well. Cover and cook on low heat for 6 to 8 hours, or until pork is very tender. Raise slow cooker temperature to high.

Mix cornstarch with ¼ cup stock until smooth. Add to stew, stirring constantly. Cook for 10 to 15 minutes, stirring frequently, until thickened.

NORTHERN ITALIAN PORK STEW

Servings: 6–8

Slow cooking makes the pork fall-apart tender and delicious with Italian herbs. Serve with hot polenta for a truly Italian meal.

2 tbs. olive oil
3 lb. pork stew meat
$1/2$ lb. pancetta, chopped
1 yellow onion, chopped
2 cloves garlic, minced
$1/2$ tsp. dried basil
1 tsp. dried oregano
$1/2$ cup chopped fresh flat-leaf parsley
1 can (14 oz.) ready-cut tomatoes
$1/2$ cup red wine

Heat oil in a large skillet over medium-high heat. Add pork and cook until browned on all sides. Transfer cooked meat to the slow cooker. Add pancetta to skillet and sauté until it begins to brown. Transfer pancetta to slow cooker.

Add all remaining ingredients to slow cooker and stir to mix well.

Cover and cook on low heat for 8 hours, or until pork is fall-apart tender.

CHICKEN AND DUMPLINGS

Servings: 6–8

You'll love the old-fashioned taste of chicken and vegetables cooked in a creamy sauce. The only tricky part about this recipe is the cooking time for the dumplings. Depending on your slow cooker, this could take anywhere from 15 to 45 minutes.

1/4 cup vegetable oil
1 chicken, cut into 8 pieces
1 yellow onion, sliced
1/2 lb. white mushrooms, thickly sliced
2 carrots, cut into 1-inch pieces
2 stalks celery, cut into 1-inch pieces
1 cup corn kernels, frozen, canned or fresh
1 cup peas, prefer frozen, but canned may be used
1 can (10.5 oz.) cream of celery soup
2 cups chicken stock
1 cup commercially prepared buttermilk baking mix
1/3 cup milk or water

Heat oil in a skillet over medium heat. Add chicken, in batches if necessary, and brown on all sides. Transfer cooked chicken to the slow cooker.

Place onion, mushrooms, carrots, celery, corn and peas over chicken. In a small bowl, mix together soup and stock until smooth. Pour over vegetables and chicken. Cover and cook on low heat for 6 hours.

Mix baking mix and milk or water together until blended. Drop in 6 spoonfuls to make dumplings. Cover and cook for 15 minutes. Remove cover and check dumplings. If they are not done, cover and continue cooking until done, checking every 10 minutes.

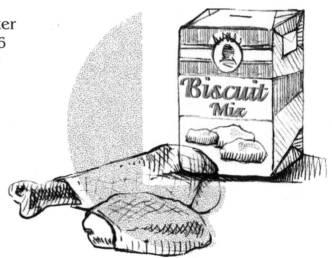

CHICKEN WITH SUN-DRIED TOMATOES

Servings: 4–6

Bits of intensely flavored tomatoes simmer with chicken and wine for a simple Italian stew. Serve with wide egg noodles and a salad.

2 tbs. olive oil
1 chicken, cut into serving pieces
2 cloves garlic, minced
1/2 cup white wine
1 1/2 cups chicken stock
1 tsp. dried basil
1/2 cup chopped sun-dried tomatoes, cut into slivers

Heat oil in a large skillet over medium-high heat. Add chicken and brown on all sides. Transfer chicken to the slow cooker.

Add garlic, wine, stock and basil to skillet. Bring to a boil, scraping up any browned bits from bottom of pan. Pour over chicken in slow cooker. Scatter sun-dried tomatoes over the top.

Cover and cook on low heat for 4 to 6 hours.

GARLIC CHICKEN

Yes, there is a lot of garlic in this recipe, but the slow cooking helps mellow the taste.

$1/2$ cup white wine
1 cup chicken stock
$1/2$ tsp. dried oregano
$1/2$ tsp. dried basil
1 chicken, cut into serving pieces
15 cloves garlic, peeled and cut in half
1 lb. tomatoes, coarsely chopped

Combine wine, stock, oregano and basil in the slow cooker. Add chicken to slow cooker. Scatter garlic over chicken and top with tomatoes. Cover and cook on low heat for 6 to 8 hours.

Remove chicken, garlic and tomatoes from slow cooker and set on a serving platter. If desired, reduce cooking liquid by pouring liquid into a medium saucepan and cooking over high heat for 10 minutes.

CRAN-APPLE CHICKEN

The bright, tart flavor of cranberries is tempered by the addition of apples to this chicken dish. You can make this any time of year by using frozen cranberries instead of fresh.

6 chicken breast halves
1 cup fresh or frozen cranberries
1 green apple, peeled, cored and sliced
2 tbs. brown sugar, packed
1 cup apple juice or cider

Place chicken at the bottom of the slow cooker. Sprinkle cranberries and apples over chicken. Mix brown sugar and apple juice together and pour over chicken and fruit. Cover and cook on low heat for 6 to 8 hours.

90   SLOW COOKER SOUPS AND STEWS

FIREBALL CHILI

Yes, this is a hot and spicy chili. VERY hot and VERY spicy! Use 5 jalapeños if you want hot and spicy; use 10 for painfully hot. There are no beans here, either. For a milder chili with beans, try California Chili, *page 92.*

2 lb. hot chorizo sausage
2 lb. ground beef
3 yellow onions, chopped
2 cloves garlic, chopped
1 can (28 oz. can) tomatoes, crushed
2 cups beef stock
1 tbs. ground cumin
1 tbs. chili powder
5–10 jalapeño chile peppers, seeded and minced

If using chorizo in links, remove sausage meat from casings and discard casings. Place chorizo and beef in a large skillet and brown meats over medium-high heat. Drain fat and add meats to the slow cooker.

Add all remaining ingredients to slow cooker. Cook on high heat for 6 hours.

CALIFORNIA CHILI

This is a medium-hot chili with lots of vegetables and beans in it. It is full of flavor but does not have too much heat. If you like the flavor but want to heat it up a bit, just add some Tabasco Sauce at the table.

3 lb. ground beef
1 lb. mild Italian sausage
2 green bell peppers, seeded and
  chopped
2 yellow onions, chopped
3 cloves garlic, chopped
4 cups tomatoes, fresh or canned

2 cups beef stock
4 tsp. ground cumin
2 tbs. chili powder
4 cans (15 oz. each) black beans
1/4 cup brown sugar, packed
1 tsp. salt

Crumble ground beef and sausage into a large skillet. Cook over medium heat until browned. Drain fat and transfer browned meat to the slow cooker.

Add all remaining ingredients to slow cooker and stir to mix. Cook for about 6 hours on high heat.

CHICKEN CHILI

Here, cubed chicken is cooked with traditional chili ingredients for a different version of chili. This makes a rather mild chili — you can adjust the heat by using regular or hot chili powder or a combination of the two.

1/4 cup vegetable oil
4 boneless, skinless chicken breast halves
1 yellow onion, chopped
2 cloves garlic, minced
2 stalks celery, chopped
3 cans (14 oz. each) tomatoes, crushed
2 cans (15 oz. each) pinto beans
1 can (4 oz.) mild green chiles, chopped
1/4 cup chili powder
2 tsp. ground cumin
1/4 cup chopped fresh cilantro

Cut chicken breasts into small (1/2-inch) chunks. Heat oil in a large skillet over medium heat. Add chicken, in batches if necessary, and cook until lightly golden. Transfer cooked chicken to the slow cooker. Add all remaining ingredients and stir to mix well. Cook for 6 hours on high heat.

PRESSURE COOKER SOUPS AND STEWS

I have heard nightmarish stories about exploding pressure cookers, with dinner all over the kitchen floors, cabinets, and ceilings. Today's pressure cookers are basically foolproof, with improved safety locks and easy-to-read pressure gauges.

Pressure cookers can cut cooking time dramatically, but it is definitely "no peek" cooking. The secret to pressure-cooking is the pressure, so once you place the lid on, you must bring the pot to the appropriate pressure, without the option of opening up the lid.

It is extremely important to be familiar with the liquid requirements of your pressure cooker. Many have a minimum amount needed to bring them to adequate pressure. If the total liquids in the recipe don't meet the minimum of your pressure cooker, add enough additional stock or water to bring it up to the minimum. You also need to be careful not to overload your pressure cooker.

When cooking bean soups, if you overcook the beans they will dissolve due to the pressure. If you like your beans whole, make sure to time the cooking exactly. If you like your bean soups a bit smoother, cook for an additional 5 to 10 minutes.

Special note: Instructions have been given at the end of each recipe for stove-top or slow cooker options.

96 Creamy Fish Chowder

98 White Bean and Basil Soup

99 Broccoli Chowder

100 Real Russian Borscht

101 Chicken Rice Soup

102 All Vegetable Stew

103 Spiced Mexican Vegetable Stew

104 Black Bean Turkey Chili

106 Porcupine Meatballs

108 Vegetarian Chili

109 Old-Fashioned Pork and Beans

110 Creole Chicken

111 Greek Lemon Chicken

112 4-Spice Chicken Curry

113 Chicken With Oranges

114 California-Style Fish Stew

115 Beef Stew Provençal

116 Beef With Black Beans

CREAMY FISH CHOWDER

Servings: 4

Cooking any fish stew or soup in a pressure cooker helps get dinner on the table fast — and you get a great-tasting meal, without tough pieces of overcooked fish. To keep the red pepper from "bleeding" its color into the soup: after chopping, rinse in cold water and pat dry. Keep on paper towels until ready to add to the soup.

1 lb. cod fillets, cut into $1/_2$-inch pieces
1 yellow onion, minced
3 stalks celery, chopped
1 lb. thin-skinned potatoes, scrubbed and chopped
3 cups fish or vegetable stock
1 cup heavy cream
1 cup corn kernels, fresh or frozen
$1/_2$ red bell pepper, seeded and chopped

Combine fish, onion, celery, potatoes and stock in the pressure cooker. Stir to mix well.

Secure pressure cooker lid. Place over high heat and bring pressure up to high. Cook at high pressure for 5 minutes. Reduce pressure and release lid.

Add cream, corn and red bell pepper. Continue to cook, uncovered, for 5 minutes or until heated through.

STOVETOP METHOD

Combine fish, onion, celery, potatoes and stock in a large stockpot. Stir to mix well. Bring to a boil and reduce heat to low. Cover and simmer for 20 minutes or until potatoes are tender. Add cream, corn and red bell pepper. Continue to cook, uncovered, for 5 minutes or until heated through.

WHITE BEAN AND BASIL SOUP

This bean soup has the Italian flavors of fresh basil and ripe tomatoes added at the end. They give this hearty soup a fresh taste and texture. Pass freshly grated Parmesan cheese or Caesar-flavored croutons.

1 lb. dried great Northern beans	6 cups chicken or vegetable stock
1 yellow onion, minced	1 tsp. garlic salt
3 cloves garlic, minced	2 cups freshly chopped tomatoes
1 russet potato, peeled and chopped	$1/4$ cup finely chopped fresh basil

Combine beans, onion, garlic, potato, stock and salt in the pressure cooker. Stir to mix well. Secure pressure cooker lid. Place over high heat and bring pressure up to high, about 15 minutes. Cook at high pressure for 35 minutes. Reduce pressure and release lid.

Stir in tomatoes and basil. Serve immediately.

SLOW COOKER METHOD

Soak beans overnight. Rinse and drain beans. Add beans and all remaining ingredients to the slow cooker. Cover and cook over medium heat for 6 to 8 hours, or until beans are tender. Stir in tomatoes and basil. Serve immediately.

BROCCOLI CHOWDER

I like to use only the stalks for this soup, but you can use either stalks and florets or just florets. Top this with grated cheddar cheese.

¼ cup butter
1 yellow onion, chopped
3 medium potatoes, peeled and
  chopped

1 lb. broccoli, chopped
6 cups chicken stock
½ tsp. salt
½ cup heavy cream

Melt butter in the pressure cooker. Add onion and sauté until onion begins to brown. Add potatoes, broccoli, stock and salt. Stir to mix well. Secure pressure cooker lid. Place over high heat and bring pressure up to high. Cook at high pressure for 4 minutes. Reduce pressure and release lid. Stir in cream and serve immediately.

STOVETOP METHOD

Melt butter in a stockpot. Add onion and sauté until onion begins to brown. Add potatoes, broccoli, stock and salt.

Stir to mix well. Place over high heat and bring to a boil. Reduce heat to low, cover and simmer for 15 minutes or until broccoli and potatoes are tender. Stir in cream and serve immediately.

REAL RUSSIAN BORSCHT

This hearty soup is close to a stew. The tiny bits of beef make this soup heartier than the usual interpretation. It is an excellent way to use up some leftover roast.

6 cups beef stock
2 cups minced cooked beef
1 cup shredded carrots
1 lb. beets, peeled and chopped
1 1/2 cups shredded cabbage

1 yellow onion, minced
1 can (14 oz.) stewed tomatoes, crushed
1 bay leaf

Combine all ingredients in the pressure cooker. Stir to mix well. Secure pressure cooker lid. Place over high heat and bring pressure up to high. Cook at high pressure for 10 minutes. Reduce pressure and release lid. Remove bay leaf before serving.

STOVETOP METHOD

Combine all ingredients in a large stockpot. Stir to mix well. Bring to a boil over high heat, cover and reduce heat to low. Simmer for 30 to 45 minutes, stirring occasionally. Remove bay leaf before serving.

CHICKEN RICE SOUP

Servings: 4–6

This cooks so fast you'll never use canned chicken rice soup again! If your chicken breasts are slightly frozen, it will be easier to cut them into thin strips and then into tiny pieces.

1/2 cup uncooked white rice
6 cups chicken stock
2 boneless, skinless chicken breast
   halves, cut into tiny pieces

1 yellow onion, minced
1 cup chopped celery
2 carrots, chopped
1/2 tsp. salt

Combine all ingredients in the pressure cooker. Stir to mix well. Secure pressure cooker lid. Place over high heat and bring pressure up to high. Cook at high pressure for 10 minutes. Reduce pressure and release lid.

STOVETOP METHOD

Combine all ingredients in a stockpot. Stir to mix well. Bring to a boil over high heat and reduce heat to low. Cover and simmer until rice is tender, about 20 to 25 minutes.

ALL VEGETABLE STEW

This stew bridges the gap between soups and stews, since it can be called either one. It's a great vegetarian meal when served with some dark bread and butter.

1 yellow onion, thickly sliced
2 cloves garlic, minced
6 red-skinned potatoes, cut into chunks
2 carrots, cut into 2-inch pieces
4 medium turnips, peeled and cut into chunks

1/2 lb. green beans, cut into 2-inch pieces
1/2 lb. tiny white mushrooms or sliced mushrooms
2 cups vegetable or chicken stock
2 bay leaves
1 cup white wine

Combine all ingredients in the pressure cooker. Stir to mix well. Secure pressure cooker lid. Place over high heat and bring pressure up to high. Cook at high pressure for 4 minutes. Reduce pressure and release lid.

STOVETOP METHOD

Combine all ingredients in a stockpot. Stir to mix well. Bring to a boil over high heat and reduce heat to low. Cover and simmer until potatoes are tender, about 20 to 25 minutes.

SPICED MEXICAN VEGETABLE STEW

Servings: 4–6

The use of cinnamon and cloves in this recipe doesn't add sweetness — it gives a depth to the rich stock for the vegetables to stew in. If you must have meat in this stew, add a couple of chopped cooked chicken breast halves to the pot.

3 yellow crookneck squash
1 yellow onion, chopped
1 clove garlic, chopped
$\frac{1}{2}$ tsp. cinnamon
$\frac{1}{4}$ tsp. ground cloves
1 bay leaf

4 red-skinned potatoes, cut into chunks
2 cups vegetable or chicken stock
2 cups chopped tomatoes
1 small head cauliflower, separated into medium florets
2 cups corn kernels, fresh or frozen

Cut squash into 1-inch pieces. Combine all ingredients in the pressure cooker. Stir to mix well. Secure pressure cooker lid. Place over high heat and bring pressure up to high. Cook at high pressure for 4 minutes. Reduce pressure and release lid. Remove bay leaf before serving.

STOVETOP METHOD

Combine all ingredients in a stockpot. Stir to mix well. Bring to a boil over high heat and reduce heat to low. Cover and simmer until potatoes are tender, about 20 to 25 minutes. Remove bay leaf before serving.

BLACK BEAN TURKEY CHILI

Servings: 4–6

Here you use the pressure cooker in two ways; first as a skillet to brown the meat and onions; then as a pressure cooker to finish the cooking.

1 lb. ground turkey
1 yellow onion, chopped
2½ lb. black beans
2 tsp. garlic salt
2 tbs. sugar
1 tbs. chili powder
1 tsp. dried red pepper flakes
2 tsp. ground cumin
1 tsp. paprika
1 can (15 oz.) ready-cut tomatoes
7 cups chicken stock or water
2 tbs. vegetable oil

Brown turkey in the pressure cooker over medium-high heat. Drain any fat. Add onion and continue cooking until onion is beginning to brown.

Add all remaining ingredients to pressure cooker. Stir to mix well. Secure pressure cooker lid. Place over high heat and bring pressure up to high, about 15 minutes. Cook at high pressure for 45 minutes. Reduce pressure and release lid.

STOVETOP METHOD

Soak beans overnight. Brown turkey in a Dutch oven or stockpot over medium-high heat. Drain any fat. Add onion and continue cooking until onion is beginning to brown. Rinse and drain beans. Add beans and all remaining ingredients to pot. Cover and cook over medium heat for 2 to 3 hours, or until beans are tender.

PORCUPINE MEATBALLS

Servings: 4

I think every pressure cooker comes with a recipe for porcupine meatballs. This version is more like a meatball stew, rather than just some meatballs.

1 lb. ground beef or ground turkey
½ cup uncooked white rice
¼ cup minced yellow onion
½ tsp. garlic salt
1 egg
¼ cup ketchup
3 cups spaghetti sauce
1 cup beef stock
1 large zucchini, cut into 1-inch pieces

Mix together ground beef or turkey, rice, onion, garlic salt, egg and ketchup. Shape into meatballs about 2 inches in diameter.

Mix spaghetti sauce and beef stock together in the pressure cooker. Place meatballs in a single layer in sauce. Place zucchini on top of meatballs.

Secure pressure cooker lid. Place over high heat and bring pressure up to high. Cook at high pressure for 7 minutes. Remove from heat and let pressure drop naturally before opening. Check for doneness by cutting a meatball in half and checking that rice is tender. If not, secure lid again and cook for another minute or two at high pressure.

STOVETOP METHOD

Mix together ground beef or turkey, white rice, onion, garlic salt, egg and ketchup. Shape into meatballs about 2 inches in diameter.

Mix spaghetti sauce and beef stock together in a large deep skillet or pot. Place meatballs in a single layer in sauce. Place zucchini on top of meatballs. Cover and cook over medium-low heat for 30 minutes. Check for doneness by cutting a meatball in half and checking that rice is tender. If not, return to heat and cook for another 5 minutes.

VEGETARIAN CHILI

This has no meat and no chicken — just a lot of beans and vegetables in a rich and spicy stock. Do not omit the vegetable oil: it helps to control foaming of the beans, which can clog your pressure cooker's vent.

1 green bell pepper, seeded and
   chopped
2 cups chopped white mushrooms
2 zucchini, chopped
3 cloves garlic, minced
1 yellow onion, chopped
2½ cups dried pinto or black beans

2 tbs. vegetable oil
6 cups vegetable stock or water
1 tbs. chili powder
2 tsp. ground cumin
½ tsp. freshly ground black pepper
1 tsp. garlic salt
1 can (15 oz.) puréed tomatoes

Combine all ingredients in a large (6-quart or more) pressure cooker. Mix well. Secure pressure cooker lid. Place over high heat and bring pressure up to high, about 15 minutes. Cook at high pressure for 45 minutes. Reduce pressure and release lid.

SLOW COOKER METHOD
Soak beans overnight. Rinse and drain beans. Combine all ingredients in the slow cooker. Cover and cook on high heat for 6 to 8 hours, until beans are tender.

OLD-FASHIONED PORK AND BEANS

Servings: 6–8 as a side dish,
4–6 as a main dish

This can be a side dish with barbecue, or a meal in itself when served with a salad and some fresh hot cornbread.

1 lb. pinto beans
1 yellow onion, minced
10 cups water
1 cup light molasses or honey

2 tsp. salt
1/2 tsp. ground cloves
1/2 lb. salt pork, cut into 1/2-inch cubes
2 tbs. vegetable oil

Combine all ingredients in a large (6 quart or more) pressure cooker. Mix well. Secure pressure cooker lid.

Place over high heat and bring to high pressure. Cook at high pressure for 45 minutes. Reduce pressure and release lid.

SLOW COOKER METHOD

Soak beans overnight. Rinse and drain beans. Combine all ingredients in the slow cooker. Cover and cook on high heat for 6 to 8 hours, until beans are tender.

CREOLE CHICKEN

Servings: 4–6

If you like a bit of heat to your Creole foods, increase the amount of hot pepper sauce to taste.

2 tbs. vegetable oil
1 chicken, cut into serving pieces
1 yellow onion, coarsely chopped
3 stalks celery, coarsely chopped
1 green bell pepper, coarsely chopped
2 cloves garlic, minced
$\frac{1}{2}$ tsp. dried thyme

$\frac{1}{2}$ tsp. dried basil
$\frac{1}{2}$ tsp. Tabasco Sauce or other hot pepper sauce
1 cup chicken stock
2 cups freshly chopped tomatoes
1 cup sliced okra, optional

Combine all ingredients in the pressure cooker. Stir to mix well. Secure pressure cooker lid.

Place over high heat and bring to high pressure. Cook at high pressure for 8 minutes. Reduce pressure and release lid.

STOVETOP METHOD

Heat oil in a Dutch oven or a large skillet over medium heat. Add chicken and cook until browned on all sides. Add all remaining ingredients. Mix well. Cover and simmer over low heat for 30 minutes.

GREEK LEMON CHICKEN

This chicken stew goes great with couscous and a spinach salad with crumbled feta cheese. Use either ripe black olives or kalamata olives if you prefer.

1/4 cup olive oil
1 chicken, cut into serving pieces
2 cloves garlic, minced
1 cup chicken stock

1/4 cup freshly squeezed lemon juice
1 tsp. dried oregano
1 cup pitted black olives

Heat oil in the pressure cooker over medium heat. Add chicken and cook until browned on all sides. Add garlic, stock, lemon juice and oregano. Mix well. Secure pressure cooker lid.

Place over high heat and bring to high pressure. Cook at high pressure for 8 minutes. Reduce pressure and release lid.

Place chicken on a serving platter with juices. Sprinkle olives on top and serve.

STOVETOP METHOD

Heat oil in a Dutch oven or large skillet over medium heat. Add chicken and cook until browned on all sides. Add garlic, stock, lemon juice and oregano. Mix well. Cover and simmer over low heat for 30 minutes.

Place chicken on a serving platter with juices. Sprinkle olives on top and serve.

4-SPICE CHICKEN CURRY

Servings: 6

This curry is not made with commercially prepared curry powder, but a simple 4-spice blend.

6 chicken breasts, cut into 2-inch pieces
2 yellow onions, cut into large chunks
1 can (15 oz.) whole baby corn
3 carrots, cut into 2-inch pieces
1 1/2 tsp. ground cumin

2 tsp. ground coriander
1/2 tsp. ground ginger
1 tsp. ground turmeric
2 cups chicken stock
1/2 tsp. salt

Combine all ingredients in a large pressure cooker. Mix well. Secure pressure cooker cover.

Place over high heat and bring to high pressure. Cook at high pressure for 9 minutes. Reduce pressure and release lid.

SLOW COOKER METHOD

Combine all ingredients in the slow cooker. Cover and cook on low heat for 4 to 6 hours.

CHICKEN WITH ORANGES

This is a sweet glazed chicken made with freshly squeezed orange juice, orange marmalade and canned Mandarin oranges. Serve with wild rice.

2 tbs. vegetable oil
1 chicken, cut into serving pieces
1/2 cup chicken stock

1/2 cup freshly squeezed orange juice
1/4 cup orange marmalade
1 can (4 oz.) Mandarin oranges

Heat oil in the pressure cooker over medium heat. Add chicken and cook until browned on all sides. Add stock, orange juice and marmalade and stir to mix. Secure lid on pressure cooker.

Place over high heat and bring to high pressure. Cook at high pressure for 8 minutes. Reduce pressure and release lid.

Place chicken on a serving platter with juices. Sprinkle mandarins on top and serve.

STOVETOP METHOD

Heat oil in a Dutch oven or large skillet over medium heat. Add chicken and cook until browned on all sides. Add stock, orange juice and marmalade. Mix well, reduce heat to low, cover and simmer for 30 minutes.

Place chicken on a serving platter with juices. Sprinkle Mandarin oranges on top and serve.

CALIFORNIA-STYLE FISH STEW

Servings: 6–8

This light fish stew works well in a pressure cooker, because the fish cooks quickly without breaking apart.

1 lb. halibut, cod or pollock
1/4 cup white wine
2 tbs. freshly squeezed lemon juice
2 cloves garlic, minced
1/2 cup chopped fresh flat-leaf parsley

1/2 tsp. dried basil
3 stalks celery, cut into chunks
1 yellow onion, chopped
1 cup sliced mushrooms
2 cups fish or vegetable stock

Cut fish into 6 or 8 pieces. Place all ingredients in the pressure cooker. Secure lid on pressure cooker. Place over high heat and bring to high pressure. Cook at high pressure for 4 minutes. Reduce pressure and release lid.

STOVETOP METHOD

Place all ingredients in a large stockpot. Cover and bring to a boil over high heat. Reduce heat to low and simmer for 10 minutes.

BEEF STEW PROVENÇAL

Servings: 6–8

You can have all the flavors of a slow-cooked French stew in about half an hour. Serve with some parsley potatoes and a glass of your favorite red wine.

3 lb. beef stew meat
2 cups red wine
2 cloves garlic, minced
1 tsp. dried thyme
1 tsp. dried rosemary
3 anchovy fillets, minced

1/2 tsp. salt
2 carrots, cut into 2-inch pieces
1 yellow onion, cut into chunks
1/2 cup chopped, pitted kalamata
   olives, optional

Combine all ingredients in the pressure cooker and stir to mix. Secure lid on pressure cooker. Place over high heat and bring to high pressure. Cook on high pressure for 15 minutes. Let pressure drop naturally (about 10 to 15 minutes) and release lid.

If beef is not fork-tender, replace lid, bring to high pressure again and cook for another 5 minutes. Let pressure drop naturally before opening.

SLOW COOKER METHOD

Combine all ingredients in the slow cooker. Cover and cook on low heat for 8 hours, until beef is fork-tender.

BEEF WITH BLACK BEANS

This Asian-flavored stew cooks as fast as a stir-fry dish. Start some white rice cooking and then prepare the beef. Also, you'll want to purchase fermented black beans, not the premade sauce, for this dish. You can find fermented black beans in the Asian food section of most supermarkets.

2 lb. beef stew meat
$1/4$ cup fermented black beans
$1/4$ cup dry sherry or white wine
$1/2$ cup beef stock
1 clove garlic, minced
1 can (4 oz.) sliced water chestnuts, drained
5 medium tomatoes, coarsely chopped
3 green onions, slivered

Combine all ingredients, except green onions, in pressure cooker and stir to mix. Secure lid on pressure cooker. Place over high heat and bring to high pressure. Cook at high pressure for 15 minutes. Let pressure drop naturally (about 10 to 15 minutes) and release lid.

If beef is not fork-tender, replace lid and bring to high pressure again, and cook for another 5 minutes. Let pressure drop naturally before opening.

Transfer stew to a serving bowl or platter and sprinkle green onions on top.

SLOW COOKER METHOD

Combine all ingredients in the slow cooker. Cover and cook on low heat for 8 hours, until beef is fork-tender.

Transfer stew to a serving bowl or platter and sprinkle green onions on top.

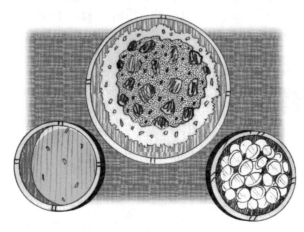

OVEN-COOKED SOUPS AND STEWS

A stew doesn't have to contain bite-size pieces of meat or vegetables. Slow cooking in the oven is an ideal way to stew larger cuts of meat and poultry, with minimum supervision. There will be evaporation, though, so make sure enough liquid is used.

Oven soups are a bit like slow cooker soups, in that you'll usually combine all your ingredients at the beginning and then let them cook together. The oven has a big advantage over the slow cooker — more heat. If you do not need the convenience of being away from the kitchen for a long period of time, and economy or conservation of fuel is not an issue, choose the oven instead of the slow cooker.

120   Peasant Potato Soup
121   Winter Squash Soup
122   Mexican Squash and Potato Soup
123   Apple and Red Cabbage Soup
124   Roasted Tomato Soup
125   Curried Lentil Soup
126   Mediterranean Beef Soup

127   Mexican Pork Chops
128   Green Chile Chicken
129   Beans and Bacon
130   Chunky Beef Chili With Beans
132   Short Ribs in Sherry
133   Beef With White Wine
134   Crab and Shrimp Jambalaya
135   Asian Lamb Stew
136   Cassoulet
138   Roasted Vegetable Ratatouille
140   Veal in Wine
141   Baked Beef Stroganoff
142   Mushroom Beef Stew With Dumplings
144   Sunday Night Beef Stew
145   Spareribs With Sauerkraut and Apples
146   Lamb and Lentil Stew
147   Pork Curry
148   Jamaican Chicken Stew
149   Chicken Stew With Vegetables

PEASANT POTATO SOUP

This version of potato soup is not puréed but has bits of potato in a slightly thickened stock.

3 medium potatoes, peeled and diced
1 carrot, chopped
½ yellow onion, minced
2 medium tomatoes, chopped
2 cups finely chopped garlic sausage or kielbasa
3 tbs. butter
3 tbs. flour
8 cups beef or chicken stock

Heat oven to 400°.

Place potatoes, carrot, onion, tomatoes and garlic sausage in a large, covered casserole dish or Dutch oven.

In a medium saucepan, melt butter over medium heat. Add flour and whisk until smooth. Add stock, stirring constantly. Bring stock to a boil and cook for 5 minutes. Pour hot stock mixture over vegetables in casserole dish. Cover and bake for 90 minutes.

WINTER SQUASH SOUP

Servings: 6–8

You can use any hard winter squash for this soup, even pumpkin. A nice variation of this soup is to cook only the squash, leeks and stock together and then puree them until smooth. The ham is added to the soup after pureeing.

3½ lb. hard winter squash
2 large leeks, white part only, thinly sliced
8 cups chicken stock
2 cups finely chopped smoked ham
½ tsp. salt

Heat oven to 400°.
Peel, seed and finely chop squash.
Combine all ingredients in a large, covered casserole dish. Bake for 2 hours.

MEXICAN SQUASH AND POTATO SOUP

Servings: 4–6

Spicy chorizo sausage flavors this potato and squash soup. You can use either mild or hot chorizo, whichever you prefer for heat. Serve with lots of tortilla chips.

1 lb. chorizo sausage
1 medium butternut squash, about 2½ lb.
2 large russet potatoes
2 cloves garlic, minced
6 cups chicken stock

Heat oven to 400°.

Place sausages in a medium skillet and cook over medium heat until lightly browned, about 10 minutes. Remove from pan and let cool until easy to handle. Slice sausages into ¼-inch-thick slices. Place sausage slices in a covered casserole dish.

Peel and seed squash. Finely chop squash and add to casserole dish. Peel and finely chop potatoes. Add potatoes, garlic and stock to casserole dish and stir to mix.

Cover and bake for 2 hours.

APPLE AND RED CABBAGE SOUP

Servings: 6–8

This slightly sweet soup is perfect for fall and winter meals. You can make it heartier by adding some cooked chicken or pork.

3 green apples, peeled, cored and coarsely chopped
4 cups coarsely chopped red cabbage
1 yellow onion, chopped
2 carrots, chopped
8 cups chicken stock
$1/4$ cup brown sugar, packed

Heat oven to 400°.
Combine all ingredients in a large, covered casserole dish. Cover and bake for 2 hours, or until apples and cabbage are very tender.

ROASTED TOMATO SOUP

Servings: 4–6

This does require a bit of tending, as you first roast the tomatoes and onions and then add the stock and other ingredients. Finally, just before serving, puree the soup. But the work is well worth it, as the soup has an incredible, deep tomato flavor. This is a great way to use your summer tomato harvest.

3 lb. tomatoes, halved
1 yellow onion, thickly sliced
1/2 cup olive oil
5 cups chicken or vegetable stock
1 cup white wine
1 tsp. garlic salt
1 tsp. dried oregano

Heat oven to 400°.

Place tomatoes (cut-side up) and onion slices on a large cookie sheet. Drizzle with olive oil. Roast until tomatoes are browned, about 1 hour.

Place tomatoes and onions in a large covered casserole. Pour stock and wine over vegetables and sprinkle garlic salt and oregano on top. Cover and bake for 30 minutes.

Puree soup in batches until smooth. Serve immediately.

CURRIED LENTIL SOUP

Servings: 6–8

This is a very filling soup without meat. You can also use vegetable stock for a vegetarian version

2 russet potatoes, peeled and chopped
2 carrots, peeled and chopped
2 stalks celery, chopped
12 oz. lentils
2 cloves garlic, minced
8 cups chicken or beef stock
2 tbs. curry powder
1 tsp. salt

Heat oven to 400°.

Combine all ingredients in a large, covered casserole dish. Cover and bake for 1 hour, or until lentils and potatoes are very tender.

MEDITERRANEAN BEEF SOUP

Servings: 4–6

Take time to cut the beef into the tiniest pieces you can and you will get a soup that is almost a stew in every bite.

1 lb. beef stew meat
$1/4$ cup olive oil
1 can (16 oz.) garbanzo beans
1 cup chopped zucchini
1 can (16 oz.) tomatoes, chopped
3 large carrots, peeled and chopped
6 cups beef stock
$1/2$ tsp. salt
$1/4$ tsp. freshly ground black pepper
1 bay leaf

Heat oven to 400°.

Cut beef into tiny pieces, no more than $1/4$-inch dice. Heat oil in a large skillet over medium heat. Add beef and stir to coat in oil. Cook until browned, about 15 to 20 minutes. Transfer beef to a covered casserole dish.

Add all remaining ingredients to casserole dish. Stir to mix. Cover and bake for 1 hour. Remove bay leaf before serving.

MEXICAN PORK CHOPS

Servings: 4

Thick-cut pork chops stew in a bold and spicy stock flavored with cumin and red pepper flakes.

2 tbs. olive oil
4 thick-cut pork chops, about 1-inch thick
1 yellow onion, sliced
6 cloves garlic, minced
4 cups chicken stock
1 tsp. ground cumin
1/2 tsp. red pepper flakes

Heat oven to 450°.

Pour olive oil into a 9-x-9-inch baking dish. Place in oven for 10 minutes to heat.

Place chops in hot oil in baking dish. Bake for 15 minutes to brown meat. Turn chops over and bake for another 15 minutes.

Remove baking dish from oven and add onions and garlic to pork. Add stock to pan; add cumin and red pepper flakes. Stir to mix. Cover tightly with foil and return to oven. Reduce heat to 400° and bake for 2 to 2 1/2 hours, or until meat is fork-tender.

GREEN CHILE CHICKEN

Mild green chiles and tomatoes make a sauce for this chicken stew. This dish is Mexican in flavor but very mild, with minimal heat.

1/4 cup vegetable oil
1 chicken, cut into serving pieces
2 cloves garlic, minced
1 can (28 oz.) tomatoes
2 cans (4 oz. each) mild green chiles, chopped
1 tbs. ground cumin
1/2 cup white wine

Heat oven to 375°.

Heat oil in a large skillet over medium heat. Add chicken and cook until browned on all sides. Transfer chicken to a covered casserole dish or 9-x-13-inch baking dish.

In a medium bowl, mix together garlic, tomatoes, chiles, cumin and wine. Pour over chicken. Use a lid or foil to cover and bake for 1 hour, or until chicken is tender.

BEANS AND BACON

When you have lots of bacon and vegetables surrounding the beans, this is more than just a side dish. I like to use a light-tasting beer, but feel free to use your favorite.

½ lb. bacon
1 yellow onion, finely chopped
1 jalapeño chile pepper, seeded and
   minced
5 cups water

1 lb. pinto or black beans
1 bottle (12 oz.) beer
1 cup finely chopped celery
1 cup chopped tomatoes
1 cup frozen or canned corn kernels

Heat oven to 350°.

Fry bacon in a medium skillet until crisp. Drain all but 2 tbs. of the fat from skillet and add onion and jalapeño pepper. Sauté until onion is translucent, about 5 minutes.

Crumble bacon into a large, covered casserole dish. Add cooked onion, pepper, water, beans, beer, celery, tomatoes and corn to casserole. Stir to mix. Cover and bake for 3 hours, or until beans are tender and most of liquid has been absorbed.

CHUNKY BEEF CHILI WITH BEANS

Servings: 6–8

This chili uses chunks of beef instead of ground beef. It can be served in a bowl or made into soft tacos. Top with grated sharp cheddar cheese and chopped red onions. And don't forget to pass some hot pepper sauce for those who like a big kick from their chili.

3 tbs. vegetable oil
3 lb. beef stew meat
2 yellow onions, chopped
2 cloves garlic, minced
1 can (28 oz.) tomatoes
1 cup beef stock
1 tbs. chili powder
1 tsp. ground cumin
1 tsp. cayenne pepper
1 tsp. salt
2 cans (16 oz. each) kidney, pinto
  or black beans

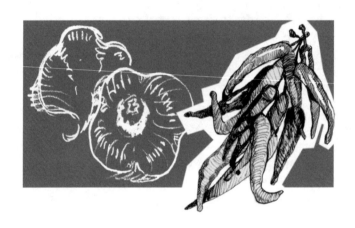

Heat oven to 350°.

In a large Dutch oven, heat oil over medium-high heat. Add beef in batches and brown well on all sides. As meat browns, transfer to a large casserole dish or 9-x-13-inch baking dish. When all beef has been browned, add onions and garlic to pan. Sauté until onions and garlic begin to brown, about 5 minutes. Add vegetables to meat in dish.

Place tomatoes and their liquid in a food processor workbowl or blender container. Pulse until smooth, working in batches if needed. Add beef stock, chili powder, cumin, cayenne pepper and salt to blender and pulse to mix well. Pour tomato mixture on top of beef.

Cover and bake for 2 hours. Meat should be fall-apart tender.

SHORT RIBS IN SHERRY

Short ribs have quite a lot of fat, which will melt off during cooking. You will need to skim off this fat before serving.

2 tbs. olive oil
3 lb. beef short ribs
1 tsp. salt
1/2 tsp. pepper
2 yellow onions, thickly sliced

1 cup dry sherry
2 cups beef stock
1 clove garlic, minced
2 tbs. Worcestershire sauce

Heat oven to 450°.

Pour oil into a 9-x-9-inch baking dish and place in oven for 10 minutes. Season short ribs with salt and pepper. Place ribs in hot oil, turn to coat all sides and place in oven for 30 minutes.

Remove from oven, and add all other ingredients. Stir to mix. Cover tightly with foil and return to oven. Reduce heat to 375°, and continue to bake until meat is fork-tender, about 2 to 2 1/2 hours.

To serve, remove meat from baking dish and place in a serving bowl. Pour stewing liquid into a fat strainer and skim off fat. Pour sherry stock over ribs and serve.

BEEF WITH WHITE WINE

Combining beef with white wine instead of red give a lighter flavor to this stew.

1/4 cup vegetable oil
2 lb. boneless beef stew meat
4 cups white wine
2 tbs. grained mustard
1 can (16 oz.) tomatoes, crushed
1/2 tsp. dried thyme

Heat oven to 350°.

Heat oil in a large skillet over medium-high heat. Add beef in batches and brown well on all sides. Transfer beef to a covered casserole dish.

Add wine to pan and scrape bottom to remove any browned bits. Raise heat to high and reduce wine down to 2 cups, about 10 minutes. Add mustard, tomatoes and thyme to wine and stir to mix. Pour wine mixture over beef and stir to mix.

Bake until very tender, about 3 hours.

CRAB AND SHRIMP JAMBALAYA

Servings: 4–6

If you are from the south, please forgive this California version of jambalaya. For a more traditional jambalaya, made with pork, chicken and seafood, try the recipe for New Orleans Jambalaya, *page 46, in the "Stovetop Soups and Stews" chapter.*

2 tbs. butter
1 cup long-grain rice
1 clove garlic, minced
$1/2$ cup diced celery
$1/2$ cup chopped green bell pepper
2 cups water or vegetable, fish or
   chicken stock

$1 1/2$ cups ready-cut tomatoes
$1/2$ lb. cooked lump crabmeat
$1/2$ lb. cooked shrimp or prawns
$1/2$ tsp. salt

Heat oven to 350°.

In a medium skillet, melt butter over medium heat. Add rice and garlic and sauté until rice becomes translucent.

Place sautéed rice in a covered casserole dish. Add all remaining ingredients and gently stir to mix. Cover and bake until rice is tender, about 45 minutes.

ASIAN LAMB STEW

Stews and Asian flavors are not a frequent combination, but here they flavor tender chunks of lamb. Try this served over hot steamed rice.

2 lb. lamb chunks, about 2-inch pieces
3 cups water or stock
$1/4$ cup sherry
2 tbs. soy sauce
1 tbs. candied orange peel, chopped
1-inch piece fresh ginger, peeled and sliced

Heat oven to 350°.

Combine all ingredients in a medium-sized, covered casserole dish. Cover and bake until lamb is very tender, about $1 1/2$ to 2 hours.

Remove meat from casserole dish. Strain liquid and discard orange peel and ginger. Return meat to dish and serve.

CASSOULET

This is not the fancy duck or goose version — just a country French stew of beans and meats.

1½ lb. dry white beans
about 6 cups chicken stock
3 cloves garlic, minced
1 yellow onion, chopped
2 stalks celery, chopped
2 carrots, peeled and chopped
2 cups ready-cut canned tomatoes
8 slices bacon, chopped
1 lb. mild Italian sausage
1 lb. pork shoulder or butt, cut into 1-inch chunks
1 lb. garlic sausage, cut into 1-inch slices
½ tsp. dried thyme
1 cup white wine

Place beans in a large Dutch oven with enough stock to cover. Place over high heat and bring to a boil. Reduce heat to low and add garlic, onion, celery, carrots and tomatoes. Cover and simmer for 45 minutes. Beans should be almost tender.

While beans cook, fry bacon in a large skillet until crisp. Remove and set on paper towels to drain. Add Italian sausage to skillet and cook until done, about 10 minutes. Remove and drain. When cool enough to handle, cut into 1-inch slices. Add pork and sauté until browned, about 10 minutes. Drain off excess fat and add wine to pan, scraping any browned bits off the bottom. Return all meats to wine in skillet.

Heat oven to 450°.

When beans are done, stir meat and wine into beans. Add thyme to meat and beans. Cover and bake for 45 minutes.

ROASTED VEGETABLE RATATOUILLE

Servings: 4–6

Traditional ratatouille is made by sautéing vegetables together in a stockpot. Here the vegetables are roasted in the oven and a small amount of liquid is added at the end. Two big differences between this and the traditional recipe: the roasting brings out a lot more flavor in the vegetables; and the flavor of each vegetable is more distinct.

1 medium eggplant, peeled and cut into 1-inch cubes
2 zucchini, cut into 1-inch cubes
1 yellow onion, peeled and cut into $1/2$-inch-thick slices
1 green bell pepper, seeded and cut into 1-inch pieces
1 red bell pepper, seeded and cut into 1-inch pieces
$1/4$ cup olive oil
2 cloves garlic, minced
$1/2$ tsp. salt
2 cups peeled, chopped tomatoes
$1/2$ cup white wine
$1/2$ tsp. dried thyme
1 tsp. dried basil

Heat oven to 425°.

Place eggplant, zucchini, onion and red and green bell peppers in a large bowl. Drizzle olive oil over vegetables. Add garlic and salt and toss to coat all vegetables. Place vegetables on a large cookie sheet in a single layer (use 2 cookie sheets if they are too crowded). Place in oven and roast until vegetables are tender and beginning to brown, about 30 minutes.

Transfer cooked vegetables and any liquid to a covered casserole dish. Add tomatoes, wine, thyme and basil and stir gently to mix. Cover and return to oven. Reduce heat to 350° and bake for 30 minutes.

Serve hot, at room temperature or chilled.

VEAL IN WINE

Servings: 4–6

This stew is perfect for a special party. Since you don't have to watch it closely, you can relax while it cooks. The white wine sauce the veal cooks in is elegant but easy to make.

2 tbs. butter
1 yellow onion, chopped
1 clove garlic, minced
2 lb. veal chunks, cut into about
    1 1/2-inch pieces

2 cups white wine
2 carrots, thickly sliced
1 tsp. dried thyme
1 tsp. salt

Heat oven to 350°.

Heat butter in a medium saucepan over medium heat. Add onion and garlic and sauté until they begin to brown. Add veal to pan and cook until meat is lightly browned. Add wine and stir to loosen any browned bits on bottom of pan.

Place veal and wine mixture in a covered casserole dish. Add remaining ingredients, cover and bake for 1 1/2 to 2 hours or until meat is tender.

BAKED BEEF STROGANOFF

This classic dish is usually served on top of wide egg noodles. I like the addition of a grained mustard to the sour cream. The ingredient list calls for 1 to 3 teaspoons; you can also omit mustard completely for a lighter taste.

1/4 cup butter
2 lb. beef stew meat
2 tbs. flour
1 1/2 cups beef stock

1 cup sliced mushrooms
1 yellow onion, chopped
1 cup sour cream
1–3 tsp. grained mustard

Heat oven to 350°.

In a large skillet, melt butter over medium heat. Add beef in batches and brown on all sides. Transfer browned beef to a casserole dish.

Add flour to remaining butter in skillet and stir until smooth. Add beef stock and stir constantly until smooth and thickened. Pour stock mixture over beef and add mushrooms and onion to casserole dish. Stir to mix. Cover and bake for 1 hour or until beef is very tender.

Remove from oven. In a small bowl, mix together sour cream and mustard. Stir sour cream mixture into casserole dish until well mixed with beef and stock. Serve immediately.

MUSHROOM BEEF STEW WITH DUMPLINGS

Servings: 6–8

I like this stew because the dumplings bake in the oven, so they are a cross between dumplings and biscuits.

¼ cup flour
½ tsp. salt
2 lb. beef stew meat
¼ cup olive oil
3 cups beef stock
3 large potatoes, cubed
1 yellow onion, chopped
1 lb. white mushrooms, sliced

DUMPLINGS

1 cup flour
1 tsp. baking powder
¼ tsp. salt
2 tsp. minced fresh parsley
½ cup milk

Heat oven to 400°.

Place flour and salt in a plastic bag. Add stew meat and shake to coat. Heat olive oil in a large skillet over medium-high heat. Add beef chunks, but don't overcrowd. Brown meat on all sides and transfer to a covered casserole dish. Add stock to skillet and scrape up any browned bits on the bottom. Pour stock over meat. Add potatoes, onion and mushrooms to meat and stir to mix. Cover and bake for 2 hours, until meat is tender. Make dumpling dough while stew is baking.

Remove stew from oven. Uncover and spoon dumpling dough on top of stew, making about 6 to 8 dumplings. Return to oven uncovered and bake for 10 to 15 minutes, until dumplings are golden brown.

DUMPLINGS

In a medium bowl, mix together flour, baking powder and salt. Stir in parsley and then add milk, stirring just enough to moisten flour — do not overmix.

SUNDAY NIGHT BEEF STEW

Servings: 6–8

This has everything in it; beef, rich gravy, tons of vegetables and biscuits on top. You don't need anything else for a full and complete meal.

2 lb. beef stew meat
1 yellow onion, chopped
2 carrots, cut into 1-inch chunks
2 stalks celery, cut into 1-inch chunks
2 medium potatoes, peeled and cut into 1-inch chunks
$1/2$ cup fresh or frozen green peas
1 cup ready-cut tomatoes
2 cups beef stock
1 container refrigerated biscuit dough

Heat oven to 400°.

Combine all ingredients, except biscuit dough, in a large covered casserole dish. Cover and bake for 2 to $2^{1}/_{2}$ hours or until beef is very tender. Place biscuits on top of stew and return to oven. Bake for another 10 minutes or until biscuits are golden and done.

SPARERIBS WITH SAUERKRAUT AND APPLES

Servings: 4–6

Many people say they hate sauerkraut. The sauerkraut from a jar or can is pretty strong; rinsing it in cool water removes most of the bitter vinegar taste.

2 lb. sauerkraut
3 green apples, cored
4 lb. pork spareribs
1 cup chicken stock
1/4 cup brown sugar, packed

Heat oven to 350°.

Arrange sauerkraut on the bottom of a 9-x-13-inch baking dish. Slice apples into 1/2-inch-thick slices and place on top of sauerkraut. Cut ribs into sections, about 4 ribs per section. Place on top of apples. Pour stock over ribs and sprinkle brown sugar over ribs. Bake for 2 hours.

LAMB AND LENTIL STEW

This stew has an "old-world" taste and texture; a course, country-style bread is perfect for soaking up the tasty stock.

2 lb. lamb stew meat
2 cups lentils
3 cups beef stock
1 yellow onion, chopped
1 clove garlic, minced
1 cup chopped celery
1 cup ready-cut tomatoes

Heat oven to 450°.

Combine all ingredients in a large, covered casserole dish and bake for 1 hour. Check stew and add more stock if needed. Reduce heat to 350° and bake for another 60 to 90 minutes, until lamb is tender.

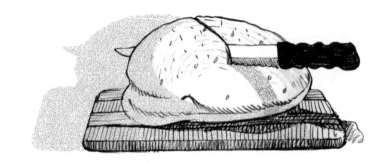

PORK CURRY

Sweet potatoes are a surprise ingredient in this curry. The sweetness of the potatoes goes well with the spicy curry sauce.

3 lb. pork stew meat
6 cups chicken stock
2 cloves garlic, minced
1 tsp. ground allspice
3 tbs. curry powder
$1/2$ tsp. cinnamon
1 yellow onion, sliced
3 large sweet potatoes, peeled and cut into 1-inch chunks
3 carrots, cut into 1-inch chunks
1 cup frozen or fresh green peas

Heat oven to 375°.

In a large skillet, brown pork in batches if necessary. Place browned meat in a large Dutch oven or covered casserole dish. Add all remaining ingredients and stir to mix. Cover and bake for 2 hours.

JAMAICAN CHICKEN STEW

This falls somewhere between a curry and Jamaican jerk: sweet, hot and spicy all at once.

2 tbs. vegetable oil
1 chicken, cut into 8 pieces
1 yellow onion, chopped
1 can (14.5 oz.) ready-cut tomatoes
1 tbs. curry powder
2 tsp. ground allspice
2 tsp. cinnamon
$1/4$ cup brown sugar, packed
$1/2$ tsp. red pepper flakes

Heat oven to 350°.

Heat oil in a large skillet over medium heat. Add chicken and brown well on all sides. Transfer chicken to a Dutch oven or covered casserole dish. Add all remaining ingredients and stir to mix well. Cover and bake for 2 hours.

CHICKEN STEW WITH VEGETABLES

Servings: 6

Here is a simple stew with a nice variety of vegetables. You can use a whole chicken, cut into pieces, or 6 leg or thigh pieces if you prefer.

1 chicken, cut into serving pieces
1 yellow onion, sliced
2 zucchini, cut into 1-inch-thick slices
4 carrots, cut into ½-inch-thick slices
1 lb. green beans, cut into 1-inch
  pieces

2 pkg (8 oz. each) frozen artichoke
  hearts
2 tomatoes, sliced
½ cup pitted black olives, halved
1 tsp. dried thyme
1 cup chicken stock

Heat oven to 350°.

In a large skillet, brown chicken pieces over medium-high heat. Place browned chicken in a large covered casserole dish or a 9-x-13-inch baking dish.

Place onion over chicken. Arrange carrots, green beans and artichoke hearts over onion. Place tomatoes in a single layer over all. Sprinkle olives on top of tomatoes. Stir thyme into stock and pour over all.

Cover with a lid or foil and bake for 1 hour.

INDEX

A

Anchovies, in beef stew Provençal
115
Apple
cranberry chicken 90
and pork stew 84
and red cabbage soup 123
with sauerkraut and spareribs
145

B

Bacon
barley and pancetta 64
and beans 129
in cassoulet 136
in Manhattan clam chowder 74
in New England clam chowder
75
in roasted corn chowder 25
Barley and beef soup 27
Barley and pancetta soup 64
Basil and white bean soup 98
Bean(s)
and bacon 129
black, and shrimp Baja soup 28

black, Cal-Mex soup 63
black, turkey chili 104
black, with beef 116
with chunky beef chili 130
chunky split pea soup 65
cooking in pressure cooker 94
curried lentil soup 125
lamb and lentil stew 146
lentil and brown rice soup 66
lentil and spinach soup 38
and pork, old-fashioned 109
soup, Tuscan 61
Texan, and sausage soup 62
white, and basil soup 98
white, in cassoulet 136
Beef
and barley soup 27
Belgian stew 81
with black beans 116
in California chili 92
chunky chili with beans 130
curry with vegetables 77
in fireball chili 91
in hamburger vegetable soup 69
Italian herbed 79

Mediterranean soup 126
mushroom stew with dumplings
142
in North Beach minestrone 14
in porcupine meatballs 106
in real Russian borscht 100
rich stew with gravy 78
round steak in steak and
mushroom stew 80
short ribs in sherry 132
stew Provençal 115
stock 7
Stroganoff, baked 141
Sunday night stew 144
sweet and smoky stew 82
with white wine 133
Black bean turkey chili 104
Black beans with beef 116
Borscht, real Russian 100
Bouillon cubes 3
Broccoli
and cheddar soup 37
chowder 99
and creamy chicken soup 22

C

Cabbage
  Chinese, and noodle soup 21
  old world soup 39
  red, and apple soup 123
Calamari, in San Francisco
  cioppino 52
Cassoulet 136
Cheddar and broccoli soup 37
Cheddar cheese soup 36
Cheese soup, cheddar 36
Chicken
  and broccoli soup, creamy 22
  cacciatore 54
  chili 93
  in Chinese cabbage and noodle
    soup 21
  and corn soup, creamy 42
  cran-apple 90
  Creole 110
  curry, red 44
  and dumplings 86
  el Cid 45
  4-spice curry 112
  garlic 89
  Greek lemon 111
  green chile 128
  gumbo 55

Jamaican stew 148
minestrone 18
in mulligatawny soup 32
mushroom noodle soup 20
with oranges 113
real old-fashioned noodle soup
  19
rice soup 101
soup, chipotle 70
and stars soup 71
stew with vegetables 149
stock 4
stock #2 6
with sun-dried tomatoes 88
in wild rice soup 68
in won ton soup 34
Chili
  black bean turkey 104
  California 92
  chicken 93
  chunky beef with beans 130
  fireball 91
  vegetarian 108
  verde 83
Chipotle chicken soup 70
Chowder
  broccoli 99
  creamy fish 96

Manhattan clam 74
New England clam 75
roasted corn 25
summer vegetable 26
Cioppino, San Francisco 52
Clam(s)
  chowder, Manhattan 74
  chowder, New England 75
  in San Francisco cioppino 52
Cod, in creamy fish chowder 96
Cod, in seafood soup 29
Corn and creamy chicken soup 42
Corn chowder, roasted 25
Crab
  in San Francisco cioppino 52
  in seafood soup 29
  and shrimp jambalaya 134
Cran-apple chicken 90
Creole chicken 110
Curried lentil soup 125
Curry
  beef with vegetables 77
  4-spice chicken 112
  pork 147
  red chicken 44

D

Dumplings with mushroom beef
  stew 142

F

Fish (see also specific kind; see also Seafood)
  chowder, creamy 96
  stew, California-style 114
  stock 8
4-spice chicken curry 112

G

Garlic chicken 89
Gravy with rich beef stew 78
Green chile chicken 128

H

Halibut, in California-style fish stew 114
Ham
  in Cal-Mex black bean soup 63
  in chunky split pea soup 65
  and potato soup 33
  smoked, in potato and spinach soup 72
  in Tuscan bean soup 61
  in winter squash soup 121
Hamburger vegetable soup 69
Herbed beef, Italian 79

I

Irish stew 48

Italian meatball soup 16

J

Jambalaya, crab and shrimp 134
Jambalaya, New Orleans 46

L

Lamb
  in Irish stew 48
  and lentil stew 146
  stew, Asian 135
  stew, Greek 51
  stew with olives and rosemary 50
Lemon chicken, Greek 111
Lentil
  and brown rice soup 66
  curried soup 125
  and lamb stew 146
  and spinach soup 38

M

Meatball soup, Italian 16
Meatballs, porcupine 106
Minestrone, chicken 18
Minestrone, North Beach 14
Mulligatawny soup 32
Mushroom
  beef stew with dumplings 142

chicken noodle soup 20
creamy soup 40
and steak stew 80
wild, and wild rice soup 41

N

Noodle(s)
  chicken mushroom soup 20
  and Chinese cabbage soup 21
  soup, real old-fashioned chicken 19

O

Olives and rosemary with lamb stew 50
Oranges with chicken 113
Oven-cooked soups and stews 1, 119-149

P

Pancetta and barley soup 64
Pasta and sausage soup 23
Pasta, in chicken and stars soup 71
Peasant potato soup 120
Pork
  and apple stew 84
  and beans, old-fashioned 109
  in cassoulet 136

Pork, *continued*
  chili verde 83
  chops, Mexican 127
  curry 147
  in Italian meatball soup 16
  Northern Italian stew 85
  spareribs, in New Orleans
    jambalaya 46
  spareribs with sauerkraut and
    apples 145
  stew, Hungarian 58
Potato
  baked, soup 73
  and ham soup 33
  peasant soup 120
  and spinach soup 72
  and squash Mexican soup 122
Prawns, in New Orleans jambalaya
  46
Prawns, in shrimp bisque 30
Pressure cooker gauges 94
Pressure cooker soups and stews
  1, 94-117

R
Ratatouille, roasted vegetable 138
Ratatouille, shrimp 76
Red snapper, in seafood soup 29
Rice, brown and lentil soup 66

Rice and chicken soup 101
Rosemary and olives with lamb
  stew 50

S
Salmon in San Francisco cioppino
  52
Salmon, in seafood soup 29
Sauerkraut with spareribs and
  apples 145
Sausage
  in California chili 92
  in cassoulet 136
  in fireball chili 91
  in lentil and brown rice soup 66
  in Mexican squash and potato
    soup 122
  in New Orleans jambalaya 46
  and pasta soup 23
  in peasant potato soup 120
  and Texan bean soup 62
Seafood (see also specific kind;
  see also Fish)
  in slow cooker 59
  soup 29
Sherry with beef short ribs 132
Short ribs in sherry 132

Shrimp (see also Prawns)
  bisque 30
  and black bean Baja soup 28
  and crab jambalaya 134
  ratatouille 76
  in San Francisco cioppino 52
  in seafood soup 29
  in won ton soup 34
Slow cooker soups and stews 1,
  59-93
Soup
  apple and red cabbage 123
  Autumn turkey 67
  Baja black bean and shrimp 28
  baked potato 73
  barley and pancetta 64
  beef and barley 27
  broccoli chowder 99
  Cal-Mex black bean 63
  cheddar and broccoli 37
  cheddar cheese 36
  chicken and stars 71
  chicken minestrone 18
  chicken mushroom noodle 20
  chicken rice 101
  Chinese cabbage and noodle 21
  chipotle chicken 70
  chunky split pea 65

Soup, *continued*
  cream of spinach 43
  creamy chicken and broccoli 22
  creamy chicken and corn 42
  creamy fish chowder 96
  creamy mushroom 40
  hamburger vegetable 69
  Italian meatball 16
  lentil and brown rice 66
  lentil and spinach 38
  Manhattan clam chowder 74
  Mediterranean beef 126
  Mexican squash and potato 122
  mulligatawny 32
  New England clam chowder 75
  North Beach minestrone 14
  old world cabbage 39
  peasant potato 120
  potato and spinach 72
  real old-fashioned chicken
    noodle 19
  real Russian borscht 100
  roasted corn chowder 25
  roasted tomato 124
  sausage and pasta 23
  seafood 29
  shrimp bisque 30
  summer vegetable chowder 26
  Texan bean and sausage 62

  toppers 2
  Tuscan bean 61
  white bean and basil 98
  wild mushroom and wild rice 41
  wild rice 68
  winter squash 121
  winter vegetable 24
  won ton 34
Spareribs with sauerkraut and
  apples 145
Spinach
  and lentil soup 38
  and potato soup 72
  soup, cream of 43
Split pea chunky soup 65
Squash and potato Mexican soup
  122
Squash winter soup 121
Steak and mushroom stew 80
Stew(s)
  all vegetable 102
  Asian lamb 135
  beans and bacon 129
  beef Provencal 115
  beef with black beans 116
  beef with white wine 133
  Belgian beef 81
  blanquette of veal 56
  California-style fish 114

cassoulet 136
chicken and dumplings 86
chicken cacciatore 54
chicken el Cid 45
chicken gumbo 55
chicken with oranges 113
chicken with sun-dried tomatoes
  88
chicken with vegetables 149
crab and shrimp jambalaya 134
cran-apple chicken 90
Creole chicken 110
garlic chicken 89
Greek lamb 51
Greek lemon chicken 111
green chile chicken 128
Hungarian pork 58
Irish 48
Italian herbed beef 79
Jamaican chicken 148
lamb and lentil 146
lamb with olives and rosemary
  50
Mexican pork chops 127
mushroom beef with dumplings
  142
New Orleans jambalaya 46
Northern Italian pork 85

Stew(s), *continued*
  old-fashioned pork and beans
    109
  porcupine meatballs 106
  pork and apple 84
  rich beef with gravy 78
  San Francisco cioppino 52
  short ribs in sherry 132
  spiced Mexican vegetable 103
  steak and mushroom 80
  Sunday night beef 144
  sweet and smoky beef 82
  veal in wine 140
Stock(s) 3–11
  beef 7
  bouillon 3
  canned 3
  chicken 4
  chicken #2 6
  fish 8
  vegetable 9
  vegetable #2 10
Stovetop soups and stews 1,
  12-59
Stroganoff, baked beef 141

Sun-dried tomatoes with chicken
  88
Swordfish, in San Francisco
  cioppino 52

T
Tomato, roasted soup 124
Turkey autumn soup 67
Turkey black bean chili 104

V
Veal, blanquette of 56
Veal in wine 140
Vegetable(s)
  baked potato soup 73
  with beef curry 77
  with chicken stew 149
  hamburger soup 69
  roasted, ratatouille 138
  spiced Mexican stew 103
  stew, all 102
  stock 9
  stock #2 10
  summer chowder 26
  winter soup 24
Vegetarian chili 108

W
White bean and basil soup 98
White beans in cassoulet 136
Wild rice and wild mushroom
  soup 41
Wild rice soup 68
Wine, veal in 140
Wine, white with beef 133
Won ton soup 34

Serve Creative, Easy, Nutritious Meals with nitty gritty® Cookbooks